Bottom Dog Press

Evensong
Contemporary American Poets on Spirituality

Edited by
Gerry LaFemina
& Chad Prevost

A Harmony Series Anthology
Bottom Dog Press
Huron, Ohio

ISBN 1-933964-01-4

Bottom Dog Press, Inc
PO Box 425/ Huron, OH 44839
http://members.aol.com/Lsmithdog/bottomdog
Lsmithdog@aol.com

Credits:
Cover Art "Evening Falls"
by Misti Hope Wudke
Book Design
by Larry Smith

See list of Acknowledgments
beginning on page 236.

We thank the Ohio Arts Council for their continued support.

Table of Contents

In Memory of Patricia Goedicke

Born June 21, 1931...Died July 14, 2006

"Please be sure to speak of my utter joy—inexpressible—but experienced ...walking barefoot over the grass around the house looking up at the stars and talking to the in-and-out cats in the shadows...walking on the same barefoot grass in the early mornings...waking in my sweet bed with the breezes blowing over and no troubles during the night...such pleasures..."

Evensong: Introductions by Gerry LaFemina and Chad Prevost

I often say that poetry is the closest thing that I have to religion, meaning that poetry, for me, is akin to prayer—it's a way of talking to the sublime, to the divine, to the transcendental. The roots of American poetry—of America itself—includes the search for transcendence, for broad understanding of spirituality, for religious "freedom." Emily Dickinson's proclamation that "some keep the Sabbath going to Church—/I keep it, staying at home" captures the sense of spiritual autonomy that is both rebels against the confines of a traditional worship and is a part of the American tradition that includes Emerson and Whitman, Waldman and Ginsberg; Rich and Baraka, and others. In the best poems of this tradition—in the best poems, in general—I not only believe that someone is talking to the divine, but that someone is conjuring it.

I grew up Roman Catholic, raised by a mother whose interest in spirituality included dinners with the yogish, astrology, past-life readings, and somewhat weekly church services; my stepmother is Jewish. I've had good friends who are Sikh, Rastafarian, Agnostic, Deist, and Atheist among other spiritual traditions. I've dabbled in a variety of spiritualities and, thanks to a great teacher, Al Sadler at Sarah Lawrence, I now consider myself an American Buddhist. Still, if you ask me what that means, I can't quite say. I've read the Bible, the gnostic gospels, the Baghavad Gita, the Q'uran, the teachings of the Buddha, and the writings of Catholic mystics such as Tielhard deChardin. I'm a religious mutt, but a spiritual pure breed.

As a contemporary poet, I find it difficult to label exactly what I am religiously, which means that I find myself disheartened and alienated by the way religion is discussed in America. Currently, there is a real *with us or against us* mentality that misses and runs counter to the point of spirituality. Asking *What Would Jesus Do?* while driving a big SUV and eating McDonald's always struck me with irony, even though the people who begged this question on bracelets and bumper stickers are, for the most part, sincere. We find intolerance counter to all understanding of the idea of "love thy neighbor" that is so central to most religious sensibilities, and so we seek a compassionate inclusion here.

As we all know the very concept of religious tolerance in America means there are numerous religious traditions being honored in this country that don't make the news. There is no Jewish television on Cable; no Islamic channel; no American Buddhist channel; no native American spirituality channel; no Quaker or Amish channels. When students sometimes ask me what religion I am, they are expecting the answer to be a Protestant denomination or, given my last name, Catholic. This anthology, *Evensong,* is a celebration of the rich spiritual tapestry that is contemporary American religious experience. If this book is flawed, recall that to be spiritual is to have faith even when one doubts, to see the flaws yet find belief.

When I write poetry, I try to give myself over to the sublime, to that which is great within, to that which knows what I don't know I know. When I participate in the writing life, I try to be giving to that which has given to me. And, let's face it, being a poet in America sometimes feels like taking a vow of poverty! But it also provides a community of others who share a belief in the power of poetry to be redemptive, to change the moral, emotional or spiritual landscapes if only for a brief moment.

Please consider this anthology a meeting house: not everyone has shown up to services, but they're all here in spirit. In the end we had to make tough choices to make this anthology happen, please read it with the generous spirit of attending church. As a gesture, a small one, Chad and I decided not to place our own work in these pages: this book is a gift to those poets and those poems, that have fed our spirits—the ones included herein and the ones who came before us. The writers here come from various spiritual traditions, but all believe in the poem and the spirit and what they can do together.

All that is left for me then to do is thank my esteemed co-editor, Chad Prevost, and publisher Larry Smith for believing in this anthology and inviting me be a part of it. I thank you for opening this collection and for thinking, meditating, and praying with us here. For sharing a belief, no matter how small, that even if one isn't sure to whom one is actually praying, that poetry is prayer.

-Gerry LaFemina

A Legacy of Spiritual Diversity

The legacy of the U.S.'s poetic tradition begins with Whitman and Dickinson. How fortunate that our poetic lineage can be traced to such distinctive personalities and writing styles, to both a man and a woman, and to two poets who were so committed to celebrating and critiquing the spiritual—both of the individual self and, especially in the case of Dickinson, the faith community. If Whitman wanted to sing and celebrate himself, it was no less a celebration of his divine connectedness to all humans, to all creatures. If Dickinson kept herself sealed off from the world most of her life, she was involved in her community at least through the bonds of her local church. And how can one not hear the rhythm of hymns through the long and common meters of her poems? If Emerson and Thoreau are known more for their philosophies, certainly they, too, carry the torch of spirituality inextricably woven to the poetic "soul" and the life project of creating.

Where does one go from there? Throughout the century, again and again, one finds in the most esteemed practitioners, a celebration of life, the divinity in all things living, and a search for meaning and order. Are such themes not intrinsically "spiritual"?

All verse, it may well be argued, is concerned on some level with the spiritual. When it seeks to make the ordinary "extraordinary," or to make the world more available to the reader, no less than when it is—or at least appears to be—irreverent or heretical. Faith, of one kind or another, is necessary for most, perhaps all, human beings. This is not to narrow the poet's role, so much as to simply admit to, and embrace, the broad scope of what it can mean to write on or about the spiritual.

Over the past several decades much of our nation's essential poetry has focused less on the individual self and, as A. Poulin, Jr. describes it in *Contemporary American Poetry*, "more on the generative and myth-making aspects of community, past and present, as well as on the spiritual resonance that informs our ongoing democratic experience..." As we come to understand, myth regulates human life as an narrative of a sacred history. Political analyst Gerhart Niemeyer suggests that myth functions, "not so much through a separate ethic, but rather through sacrifices, purification rites, initiation, marriage, birth and burial ceremonies, incantations and taboos." The nature of the poems within, then, connects us to the ancient myth, the true myth, which serves to recall us again and again to a deepened awareness of reality, to a commitment to the whole in which we participate.

It would be naïve, however, not to see deep fault lines in this "whole." Our nation finds itself in a time of war, a war, at least on the surface, of competing ideologies aligned with religious conviction. Beyond this, however, we find ideologies within our own nation in as great a schism between one another as anywhere else. Growing up as the first son of a Baptist Minister, I have experienced first hand the painful ways in which politics masquerading as theology create deep wounds even within a denomination founded upon Local Autonomy of the church, and the Priesthood of the Believer—common enough beliefs to most Protestants. This anthology invites readers to join others at the table.

One of the great wonders of poetry is its capacity for revelation. However one defines the role of verse and its relationship with the spiritual, no doubt poetry's power comes from its capacity to arrest attention, to surprise, to say something that one doesn't come across in, say, politics, journalism and advertising. Former U.S. Poet Laureate Billy Collins calls poetry, "an oasis away from public language" in an article, "Poetry's Pull Stronger in Times of Trouble." Rita Dove articulates the complexity of the craft itself when she remarks in a *Writer's Chronicle* interview (2005 October/November), "To me one of the scariest and most essential things about writing poetry is that there are a thousand ways to do it. And there are a thousand paths to explore, each leading in a different direction."

In putting together an anthology of about 30 poets which attempts to give a slice of the diverse spiritual and religious expressions of our North American poets, we have tried above all, to create an anthology that represents America's greatest spiritual asset—its diversity. Gerry LaFemina and I have invited work from poets, literally and figuratively, all over the map. An important distinction of this anthology is what the poets so generously share about belief, tradition, faith, ritual, myth, mystery, and the pursuit of the ineffable as it relates to their lives and work. From the following 30 writers, readers will find represented nearly half the states in the U.S., as well as those from Latin, Asian, African, Anglo and Native American cultures and heritages, with their corresponding wide ranges of religious and/or spiritual affiliation and expression.

We have also made room for writers at a wide variety of career stages while not compromising in selecting poems of high artistic quality. These poems demonstrate—among the "thousand ways to do it"—gifts for the music of language, a sharp eye for physical detail, a rich vocabulary, and a deep concern for the world and all who inhabit it. With the same focused attention one might give to prayer or art, we invite readers to discover what we have as this project has come into being—a sense of the presence of the divine within and above ourselves, and our deep connection to one another even in our unique diversity. It is our hope that one's own particular spiritual journey and/or religious expression might be enhanced by what one experiences within.

-Chad Prevost

Francisco Aragón

Biographical Sketch

Francisco Aragón: Shortly after getting married in the late fifties, my father emigrated to California from Nicaragua, sending for my mother six months later—just in time for her to give birth to Maria, my oldest sibling. The youngest of four, I was born and raised in San Francisco and lived on Fair Oaks Street on the border of the Mission District and Noe Valley, and so claim them both as my neighborhoods. After college, I lived and traveled in Spain, residing in Madrid for the better part of the nineties. More recently I have lived in Elkhart, Indiana and currently in South Bend, Indiana, and marvel at how Latino the Midwest is becoming.

Francisco Aragón is the author of *Puerta del Sol* (Bilingual Press, 2005). His poems and translations have appeared in various anthologies and journals. He directs Letras Latinas—the literary unit of the Institute for Latino Studies at the University of Notre Dame. A native of San Francisco and long-time resident of Spain, he resides in South Bend, Indiana. To learn more, visit: http://franciscoaragon.net/.

La Palabra

In the beginning was the Word. And the Word was made flesh and dwelt among us. The role of spirituality and my relationship to poetry could begin with these snippets from the gospel of John. And then there is San Juan de la Cruz. The Spanish poet, critic, and contemporary of Lorca, Dámaso Alonso, wrote in an essay that he believed in God because the poetry of Saint John of the Cross existed: such was his experience of those words.

Gary Snyder once said something like: "Repeating certain words aloud in a certain way can embody a kind of sacredness." He was talking about chanting, how repeating a certain word transforms it and, in the process, transforms us. That's how I aspire to experience a poem: hearing or uttering a kind of prayer.

I was raised Catholic and educated by Dominican sisters and Marianist brothers. Currently, I find myself at Notre Dame. What mostly survives is my continued attachment to the liturgy. Hearing Mass can be like entering an aesthetic realm that, if done well, engages the senses. As when I walk into the Cathedral in Santiago de Compostela in the Celtic region of Spain, and experience a liturgy that includes huge thuribles of incense swinging to and fro. The poetry that holds my interest can be a kind of communion—whether between writer and absent reader; writer and an audience the poet is reading to; or writer and absent loved one, living or dead.

It was my father who introduced me to a poem in Spanish titled "Motivos del Lobo" (Motives of the Wolf). Before I read it, I heard him paraphrase it while walking with him to a Safeway supermarket in the spring of 1997. My mother, who emigrated to San Francisco with him in the late fifties from Nicaragua, had recently passed away. But he had left home shortly before I was born, and so my siblings and I were raised in a single-parent home. After cancer claimed our mother that January in 1997, we tracked our father down. I traveled north to a small town near Chico to visit him. He told me about the poem. And though I haven't seen or spoken to him since, one might say that Darío's poem was my father's gift to me. A couple of years later, I took "Motivos del Lobo" to Dublin and spent a week re-casting it as "The Man and the Wolf."

The occasion of this anthology prompts me to venture that the poem can be a space where solace, as well as communion, is possible. Spending that intensive week with "Motivos del Lobo" was spending a week with Rubén Darío (poet from Nicaragua who died in 1916) and engaging with his particular take on a myth from the life of Saint Francis of Assisi. It was also a time of recollection, in Ireland, of those several days I was able to visit with my father nearly ten years ago in Northern California. Some seek the spiritual as an attempt at wholeness. Poetry, at times, is like that for me.

FA, April, 2006/ University of Notre Dame

The Man and the Wolf

after Rubén Darío

His heart the texture of a rose,
his tongue a swath of sky,
his manner delicate—now

chatting with what many call
a beast: the look in the eyes rabid,
black: on the skirts of the village

devoured sheep and shepherd alike.
Men skilled with iron were routed.
Fangs shredded hunting dogs

like baby lamb. So out he went
looking for his den, found him
outside it, from where the animal

lunged at the sight of him, then saw
the hand rise, heard him say:
"Peace be with you, brother wolf."

The mammal knew that gesture,
snapped out of it and froze:
"Oh, it's you." "Why,"

asked the man, "must you lead
this life? The blood your snout
spills; the grief and terror

you mete out; peasants sobbing,
who are children of God...
Does this please you? Are you

from hell, or perhaps consumed
by some eternal ire?" And the wolf,
subdued, said: "Winter is hard

and hunger worse in a freezing
forest that yields nothing to eat.
It's true: I looked for livestock

to feed on, and did, and ate
shepherds too. As for blood,
the hunter on his horse gripping

his metal pursuing boar, bear,
and deer—sheds more. I've seen scores
of them inflict wounds, torture

God's creatures. And hunger
is not what drives *them* to hunt."
To which the man responded: "Evil

exists in humans. We are born
with sin. But the simple soul of a beast
is pure. From this day on you'll have

enough to eat. And you will leave
the people of this land, and their flocks,
alone. May God appease that side

of you." "Okay, it's a deal."
"As a gesture of faith extend
your paw—let's shake on it."

The wolf did as asked and lifted
his foot. The man wrapped his
fingers around it, gently squeezed.

They headed for the village. People
could hardly believe their eyes: the wolf
strode behind the man in the robe

like a family dog, his head bowed.
Every man, woman, and child
came closer, until the whole village

had gathered in the plaza where
the man began to speak: "Let me
introduce a new neighbor," he said,

pointing to the wolf with an open
hand. "Fear him not. He is
our enemy no more. In return,

I'm going to ask that each of us
do our part and feed him. He is,
after all, a creature of God."

The village responded as one:
"So be it!" The wolf raised
his head in acknowledgement,

moving his tail from side to side,
disappeared through the gates
of a convent, the man ahead of him.

For a time the wolf was at peace
in that place. His ears would fill
with psalms—his eyes with tears.

He learned how to move with grace,
to play pranks in the kitchen.
When the man whispered his prayers,

the wolf would pass his tongue across
his sandals. Out into the street
he'd go, through the valley, over hills,

into homes, where people gave him things
to eat. To them he seemed a docile hound.
And then the man had to leave

for a time. The sweet wolf, the good
and gentle wolf vanished and went
back into the hills. The howling began

again. Once more people were filled
with fear, villages nearby with dread.
Weapons and valor were useless, the rage

never letting up, as if something
burned, smoldered inside the beast.
The day the man returned villagers

sought him out, wept their complaints
about the suffering inflicted—that
infamous creature was at it again.

A shadow passed over the man's face.
He headed for the hills to track
him down—that butcher of a wolf.

He found him at his cave. "In the name
of the Father, who sees it all, what
have you got to say for yourself?!"

As if in pain, the animal spoke,
his mouth foaming, his eyes nearly
swollen shut. "Don't come any closer...

Peace and calm were my masters
these days. Even with you gone
I visited the village. When given

scraps to eat, I chewed, swallowed
in silence, with gratitude.
But I began to see, in many homes,

how people treat each other,
embers of greed, intolerance, lies
glowing subtly in countless faces.

The weak were losers, the cruel winners.
Brother made war on brother. Male
and female were like dog and bitch,

and then they began to beat me,
considered me weak for licking
their hands and feet. I believed

you: all of creation were family—
men my siblings, oxen too, the stars
my sisters, my brothers worms.

But they picked on me, drove
me away. Their laughing was like
scalding water, re-awakening

a beast—suddenly a 'bad' wolf
is what I was, yet better than most
of them. And so the struggle

to survive took over: to defend myself,
to feed myself, like the bear does,
like the boar, who, in order to live,

must kill. So let me remain here,
wild and free. And you, my friend,
back to your people, your good

and tender deeds." The man
didn't say a word. Deep
was his gaze. Then he walked away,

tears on his cheek. His heart,
touched with desolation, offered
a prayer only the wind in the forest

could hear, carrying it skyward.

Nicaragua in a Voice

More than the poems—
the fruits that sang
their juices; dolls, feverish,
dreaming of nights,

city streets—for me it was
the idle chat between the poems:
cordial, intimate almost...
like a river's murmur

as if a village—Chontales,
Granada—could speak,
whistle, inhabit
a timbre...as if, closing

my eyes, I had it again,
once more within reach:
his voice—my father
ill, will not speak.

Robin Behn

Biographical Sketch

Robin Behn went to Oberlin College to study the flute and ended up writing a different kind of music called poems. She lives with her son and soft-coated wheaten terrier, dividing her time between Birmingham, Alabama, and Montpelier, Vermont.

Robin Behn is the author of *Paper Bird*, *The Red Hour*, and *Horizon Note*, winner of the Brittingham Prize from The University of Wisconsin Press. She also co-edited *The Practice of Poetry: Writing Exercises from Poets Who Teach*. Recipient of grants from the NEA and Guggenheim Foundation, she teaches at The University of Alabama and Vermont College.

The Name of God

Of the poems included here, "The Name of God" is the earliest. It comes from my second book, *The Red Hour*, where it is one of a number of poems of outright religious questioning. I wrote it at a time in my life when I was consciously searching for a language for the divine, even having weekly chats with the student rabbi in the small town where I then lived. I had been raised as a Unitarian, and taught from an early age that it was up to me to figure out what I did or didn't believe. Sometime shortly after writing this poem, I decided to give up my conscious search for a language for God, for a language of if-God, and, rather, to commit myself to the impossibility of it, allowing each poem to build, from scratch, a temporary scaffolding like a makeshift altar reaching toward—well, something. Rather than trying to name or arrive at mysteries in my poems, I began to locate the veil of soul making as the beginning point of language, and to start from a place well past where the mysteries had first been noted, to see how far out into that place a poem might take me. In my most recent collection,

The Yellow House, from which the rest of these poems are taken, I created an imaginary place, a yellow house, and decided to meditate on it for a few years. It became, over time, both a narrative backdrop for the lives of the characters and their journeys and reckonings, and a living entity in its own right that gave me a freedom to talk directly about the ineffable. The house not only embodied spirits but had a spirit of its own that I discovered as I kept writing. Sacred, surreal, sustaining—the yellow house became for me a place of deepening worship.The house came to me one afternoon in a kind of vision, and kept me company for years. If that's not a divine gift, I'm not sure what is. My job seemed to be to give it words, building the space over and over in my mind, a necessary and makeshift architecture for, and of, the soul. One day, the letters of the word *house* rearranged themselves into a *horse*. And so a horse walked into the house and guarded over it like a totem animal, but one with its own foibles and needs, a testament to language as a complicated crucible of the divine.

Yellow Morning

She awoke deep into the morning,
        forgiving words.

Forgiving how they want to make
        the whole world one color.

Forgiving how that color is loneliness incarnate.
        Forgiving how they persist,

building themselves an altar
        peopled with people, thinged with things,

and touched, sun or no sun, with sun:
        she awoke so deep into the morning

time had gone pungent and dim
        like the smell of an old locked trunk

stirred by a slow ray of light,
        within.

This is the dream of the woman,
        and this is the dream about the woman

another woman, her/not-her,
        woke in the middle of, and wept.

Outside, a fledgling
        —filthy lump upon a wet, black bough—

punctured daylight with its high cry,
        the sound of it shredding time

—a nest, a nest, a nest—
        until an adult the color of blood

appeared and put his blunt beak down
        into the tiny throat.

But then it woke again,
            not trusting the dream of trust,

and cried, and cried-and-cried
            —for-SA-ken, for-SA-ken—

so that an adult the color of blood rolled in the earth
            appeared and put her whole blunt beak

down into the throat and held it there
            the length of time it takes

in love, for the grail to be passed,
            and then, and then, it could sleep.

Who fed the birds?
            It happened outside of words.

Black Oil Sunflower Seed?
            Whatever. A need.

Pursuit of the Yellow House

            The way the body builds a house
                        around a grain in its own sight,
objecting to the object, mulling

            and mouthing it, washing and rubbing it,
                        making a little gem of pain
the body soothes and swaddles in a small red

            pearl it sets upon the outer grasslands
                        of the eye—
did the house arise around you

            because of something *other*, the barren
                        possible, a tender, trembling mux
that flowed from you and cooled?

Or did it first appear
in the distance—
note-on-a-staff, hand-shaped bird,

flickerings' ledger, cornice-of-a-cure—
so that you,
Manger-Monger, Dank-

Hankerer, Daffodil-Whisperer, Termite-
Diviner and Would-Be Curator
of the Secret Stair where you did and you

did and you wept and you
lay down and
no more than usual did the sun refuse you,

pursued—
with wood with wooing with words—
this casket of sun this what-you-hath-done this

deckled abyss this claw-colored *is*.
Mute vial.
Tear-on-a-string

the color of use.
Amber ampul
to contain our —all.

To set us loose.

The Name of God

You, whose name
I am trying to learn
late in my life,

is it too much to ask
the battered roses to teach me?
They keep on waving and waving

their torn sleeves
        like ladies on a dock
though the ship's long gone.

Too much to ask this grass
        darkening in rain
like the hair on my head

that a man
        once called beautiful,
that also darkens as I stand

at this fountain in the rain?
        I have always preferred
the rise and fall of predictable plots,

though this one's marred
        a little, I confess,
by random August rain.

I have wandered quite accidentally
        into the garden.
The angel here is stone—

how beautiful she must have been
        inside the marble block
where only you could see her.

Then money made the sculptor
        chip away her clothes, flick
the last chink

from the shapes called *lips*.
        Did she offer up your name then,
—a cry unplugged from rock—

or did it take the pump
        to lift that word
through the secrets of her body

and spew it out her mouth?
      Ventriloquist, what if
there is no word at all for you

except for water
            that, after I have gone,
will finally carry off

the dummy angel's body?

Above the Attic of the Yellow House There Is Another Set of Stairs

You'll know by the yellowing lowering,
and by the sheen of boxes bathed

in a broken, aureate glow, and by the weight
as of a league of yellow-throated feathers,

and by the silent spiralings
of tubes plugged at both ends,

and by the snarlings of wire
debrided to the yellow veins of the objects

you've despaired of, saved for and despaired of,
and by the single stalk and yellow bulb

about to flower downward toward
the tiny human meadow where you stand.

You can climb here any time you want.
You can sway among these ruins and runes.

Like a bee in amber, something of you stays
and the hum of you keeps climbing.

Christopher Buckley

Biographical Sketch

Christopher Buckley: I grew up in Montecito, a woodsy suburb of Santa Barbara, CA, and it was just a short bike ride or creek-walk to the sea. In the '50s and early '60s there were no crowds and traffic—no one had heard of us. Having to move away mid-life for a job in the east focused my writing on my theme of home/loss of Eden; growing up in Santa Barbara mid-century was almost beatific. Today, I live an hour north in Lompoc, tract houses on the outskirts of Santa Barbara built for nineteen thousand selling routinely for one million. I drive back each week collecting the images of home.

Christopher Buckley's most recent book is *And the Sea* (The Sheep Meadow Press, 2006). Sheep Meadow Press also published his 13th book of poetry, *Sky,* in 2004. His first book of creative nonfiction, *Cruising State: Growing Up in Southern California* was published in 1994, and a new book of nonfiction, *Sleep Walk* is out from Eastern Washington Univ. Press (2006). Over the last 25 years his poetry has appeared in such literary journals as *APR, POETRY, FIELD, The Georgia Review, The Iowa Review, TriQuarterly, The Kenyon Review, Ploughshares, The New Yorker, The Nation, The Hudson Review*.

Metaphysics

Having abandoned the orthodox and arbitrary Catholic beliefs I was brought up with by the time I was ten or eleven, I turned back unconsciously—it now seems—to a metaphysics sourced in the natural and everyday world. I grew up in Montecito, a suburb of Santa Barbara and could walk out my door and find "nature"—creeks, woods, hills, long and empty beaches. I was blessed. This was in the '50s and early '60s when Southern California had more trees than cars. In the last 25 years or so, the only formulated belief system I found probable or reasonable was Buddhism and its tangent lines of thinking. I never practiced formally; catholic school cured me of the desire to join into any group. But a Zen or Buddhist way of thinking helped me to work out day to day struggles as well as formulate arguments for my poetry that took up a metaphysical project. Concepts such as the "empty bowl" of the soul, acceptance, stepping to the side to avoid conflict, help me, in many cases, to deal with the rush of experience, longing, and the physical world in opposition to the metaphysical. I think much of the struggle of art/writing poetry is sourced in that struggle for understanding. Looking back on over thirty years of work, I find that in very large part, "soul" has been my abiding subject, and I have gone back and forth in hope and in doubt trying to find evidence of the metaphysical within the physical. Surely, the light of this world must be the light of the other world; or, that other world is daily shining within this one? We are lucky to be here.

A Little Poem About God

Inventor of trees, a first draft of the vast prairies,
He was looking for something
to direct our attention.

After a while, He specialized in birds, the light
analogies He hoped we'd pick up on
before they all disappeared.

And though you'd think birds alone would have
kept him busy, He became distracted
with the seas, the metaphor

of the blue and the invisible, the indeterminate
at every turn, the absolute subterfuge
of stars—all the possibilities

like currency, until there we were, wealthy beyond
belief, with our free will and philosophies.
But in time we grew heavy

with Time, and the sea was turquoise, green, or grey,
and there was no disposition, no indication
in the white caps or the breeze.

Occasionally, the moon traced a finger along the shore,
and we had at least, sand in common—one of the last
things slated to wear away.

A cloud hoists the sky on its back. He looks out the window
again from his great room of clouds—at some
old light, at weariness gathered

in the cypress or cedar boughs, in the arms of the wind.
Waves carry us out toward the stars, but we
are not built for eternity—we only

appreciate things we are going to lose, or have lost . . .
funny thing about human nature—we have to decide
every day what to do with our lives.

[In memory of Yehuda Amichai]

Keeping My Own Company

quien habla solo espera hablar a Dios un dia—
-Antonio Machado

After all, the afternoons are off gossiping among the pines,
and the first excursions

of stars won't start up south of here for an hour, climbing
that bright net, and there

at the far end of evening, beyond the dim light of the patio,
they will again confirm nothing

so absolute as the inattentive moon. Closer to home, jays
annotate the doubtful margins

of the oaks, and a mockingbird tells all he's learned from
trial and error—little more

than a coating of dusk on his wings to show for it. Otherwise,
I have only met up with middle age,

a man in shirt sleeves walking away, across the ruined fields,
a man who, without noticing,

crosses over to another country where the roadside grasses are still
burning at his heels, where

the same clouds clang overhead, and that ache in his back—dull
as those tin clouds—says only

that the dark is coming on. It seems improbable that more might be
revealed on a day no different

than the rest, when I have again gone dreaming the roads of my youth
with their white discouraged dust,

alongside olive and lemon groves, with roses burning beneath the sun,
a fragrant sorrow on the air.

And so I also miss the Milky Way, the swirled spangle and milt,
all the misplaced evidence of God

swimming away. Who am I talking to each evening across the table,
the candle wavering between us?

A boy with a satchel of stolen tangerines, a man sporting that
dust colored houndstooth coat

from the Thrift? Lord of the warblers, Lord of ice in the heart
of the red shouldered hawk,

Lord of dust that has settled all week in the glasses for wine, today
I desire nothing from the world.

Here I am, the same so far, heart like a weed holding on, the globe
hardly moving. And it comes to me

that I was never meant to interpret the heavens, meant for nothing
more than the minor admonishments

of wind, a scoured sky responding to the last blue petitions
of the sea, where I wish again

for a little space to breathe, where I am taken with the spindrift,
the implicit small talk of stars.

Star Apocrypha

Where stars are concerned, I am as enthusiastic
as the next one—those planets just forming

across the cosmic lot, the cold blue quasars finally

arriving after fifteen billion years,

one apparently as hopeful as the next. I think we all
came to live in this world so why

should the sea in its white glitter, fasting for the sun,
or the stutter in a line of clouds have us

thinking of death, the continuing resolution of the dark
that reads entirely across the sky? For exuberance

we have the shoal of stars, the command performance
and grand galactic archipelagos, the sea foam

and abacus of stars. Yet all the time, finite by definition—
they have done the math. On a smaller scale,

I can no longer enjoy even a small espresso without
considering the atomic consequences—

arrhythmia, free radicals and pancreatic dissolution, but
there are other examples—St. Catherine of Siena

living for years on nothing but the host of air, levitating
as purely as the stubborn light she was becoming.

Why then be on earth? Yet even I fly through the blue night
sometimes, in my astral body, light as the bread

she would not eat, and for a while there, above the palm trees
and cypresses, all things seem possible to a man,

who, though he knows his weight on earth, can, among his friends,
lift off the sidewalk, rise to the occasion of wind,

of his improbable dreaming soul, as it floats away, effortless
in its modesty, in his star-white shirt—and godwit

or sanderling, be as congenial, as satisfied to receive the sun
off the spume of waves, the gilded aura of thought

lifting from the star pine's boughs, the small contributions
to the infinite panoply, the boundless savor of light . . . .

The dove who arrives on my balcony, and paces the railing
in her flame colored feet, is not a poetic truth,

but an earthly one who stands for her grey apprehensive self,
dark unmetaphorical eye eyeing me

before she flutters off into the half mystical eucalyptus
that this morning is separating wind from wind

to no avail, and which, along with the doves, seems to
repeat the long Aramaic vowels of the Essenes

swirled through canyons of the Dead Sea, almost as old as sand.
I decipher nothing and unlike them, I give up little,

and for lasting imperfection, turn to the waves, as close to
the scroll of stars, as beyond time, as we're going to get.

Today, what more shall we believe about ourselves? Half the time
the stars go missing. Eye of the dove, dark as the unlocked

heart of space, there must be something else . . . . Starry needles
just sew and unsew the dark so that the days return—

how long has the sky been waiting for all of this to arrive?
All we are is respiration—no distance and little wind,

a verse which could quit any time—*et cum spiritu tuo*—
the last breath gone out with the wild idea of us.

Christopher Bursk

Biographical Statement

Christopher Bursk is the author of nine books, most recently *The Improbable Swerving of Atoms* (University of Pittsburgh Press) and *The First Inhabitants of Arcadia* (University of Arkansas Press). He teaches at Bucks County Community College in Pennsylvania, and has been recognized for his work with prisoners, the homeless, food banks, and women's shelters.

Belief

Although I am an atheist, my lack of faith in God has not stopped me from being a Sunday School teacher and youth group leader in my church. I believe when I sing the hymns; I believe when I take communion. I do not believe when I look at the world in all its many injustices. I do not believe when I grieve for those who have died and are dying. Lying in bed late at night, I face my own mortality and know that at some point there will be an end to me. Forever.

I do believe when I listen to a man in jail share his struggles and come to some understanding in his life. I do believe when my grandchildren and I hide under the dining room table from the wicked, wicked wizard. When I walk along at the edge of the ocean it doesn't matter what I believe. The tide still comes in.

The closest I come to prayer is when I am writing.

My spirituality does not depend on there being a God or an afterlife, neither of which I have any hopes for. I put all my faith in the language. Of course, it will let me down. It will betray me. But I still put my faith in it.

Prayer

God of the feather rubbed across a cheek,
God of the tuft of fur under a cat's chin,
finger moistened and pressed into the ear's hollow,
cluck of tongue making hoofbeats, all
brisk, clear sounds listened for
that fit the ear, folds and wrinkles,
God of lucky alignments,
God of the condom a thirteen-year-old
rolls and unrolls on his thumb.

God of tongue and groove, bevel, slide rule,
slip-knot, paperclip, the bolt's threads—
God of pipes and plugs, tumblers in a lock—

It feels like a nail is being driven
into my skull, she cried out. *My head hurt*s.
A gentle woman's brain is dead,
then her body too—
death fitting tight as those middle years of marriage,
as the ring she tugged at, that pushed against
the hard bone of her knuckle.

We stand at the grave
and try to make our feet
fill the prints dried there in the mud.

Surely there is no god of pain and disease,
only some lesser, propitiatory one
we can pray to, God of nut and bolt,
safety-pin and rubberband, God of latch and key,
sleeve and gentle tugging there,
God of the hand on the inner arm,
God of a whispered urgency, two friends at a table
talking over the sound of rain,
God of long vowels that linger in our mouths,
whose look we've come to love,
moon, piano, spider, sieve. A language
that is often a solace just to say:

cinnamon and *orange, seam* and *wrinkle*.

God of such beautiful approximations,
a saying *yes*, that will have to do,
to see it, feel it. *Yes*,
that will do

Taking Turns

Today Alisha, Sarah, Craig, Amanda, Glenn, Justin, and Todd
crowd around the time machine
and listen to the prayer inside.
Because they don't recognize the voice, they pay attention.
Then there is a shrill music.
Then they enter the darkness.

They are going back to God,
and must be scared, be in the tunnel
long enough to wish for the light.
"You are deep in the Bible,"
we tell them,
and Todd gets to knock, Glenn to open the door.

Sarah leads us into the Temple
and the children are disappointed and glad:
it is only their classroom,
they have not been led back into history
to be left and forgotten.
And Justin's father is dressed in sheepskin.

He is Eli, pretending to sleep,
and his servant Samuel is pretending to sleep.
The children hide behind the folding door,
they are quiet,
they are God today
and whisper, "Samuel, Samuel."

And the boy wakes and goes to wake his master.
Next time they shout louder, "Samuel, Samuel!'

the next time even louder.
The more they stir the boy from his heavy Biblical sleep,
the sillier they get,
and the closer to his cot and Israel.

Till they are poking Samuel,
pushing each other aside to rouse him from sleep.
"Isn't he ever going to guess
we are God?" Glenn asks. "We aren't really in ancient days,
are we?" Alisha wants to know.
She has never let go of the teacher's hand—just in case.

A very old Bible is brought out
but no one is able to read, so we just take turns
touching it.
"Are we touching time?" Todd is suspicious.
Then it is time.
The children go back into the tunnel

To the cardboard box and the prayer.
They like the darkness
now that they have been through it already.
They will come again.

De Rerum Natura

... the funeral song is mingled
With the cry of babies come to the shores of light

It's the perfect book if you're thinking of killing yourself,
but don't really want to. If you'd like to
believe in God but find Him
even more daunting than that erector set
you got one Christmas, all those complicated instructions
when really all you wanted to do was
screw one shiny metal thing to another. If despair's
your only true principle, if you're convinced
that the world's an awful place,
Lucretius won't try to sway you
from your allegiances. He provides more than enough
pestilence, war, disease

to satisfy the most confirmed pessimist:
The throat oozes black blood, the tongue drips gore,
The dogs stretch flat on the street and lay down their sick souls,
And the bodies of lifeless parents are heaped
On the lifeless bodies of children.
Yet right after *the temples become charnel houses*
there Lucretius is, on page after page,
giving lectures on meteorology, saying *Gee whiz*
in Latin, like the biggest dork on the earth,
a professor so excited about his lab experiment
he stops worrying whether the students are awake
or not. He can't get over the vacuum
that makes life so interesting:
how the atoms have to keep filling it
in new and unpredictable ways. If you want a reason
to go on living, even in the midst
of a long and protracted war, it's the magnet, that
stone at which you gape in wonder....
You can link rings in a chain suspended from it,
And sometimes you'll see five or even more
Dangle in order and sway in the light breeze
One ring depending on the next, as each
Communicates with the magnet's binding force
And clings—such potency seeps through them all.
Once you get Lucretius started,
there's no stopping him. He's like a kid fallen
so in love that nothing makes sense now
except in reference to the one he's besotted with. *Magnets!*
Remember those little dogs
that kids used to play with, pulling the white terrier
from the black, then making it fly smack into the other
as if there were no end to the pleasure
of investigation: hypotheses you had to keep testing over and over,
the air first charged with the power
of refusal, then the irresistible embrace, north seeking south.
south seeking north, crazed lovers,
the urgent kiss of metal
against metal? Were these little Scotties
really teaching boys and girls the facts of life?
Maybe kids wouldn't get so screwed up
if they kept up their religious studies

of magnetism. After all, Lucretius died only a few years
before Christ was born. Maybe the cross
is a kind of magnet. Drugs are, surely. And porn.
Maybe it's not just okay to be pulled
toward the very thing that you know
you must resist. Maybe
it's a law of physics. Open *De Rerum Natura*
to Book Six, if you are not sure
that life's worth living, if you're torn this way and that.
Look, Lucretius says, it's all possible
because there's so much space
to be filled and it gets really crowded
with all those plagues and priests
telling everyone what to believe. *But—*
how the author of The Nature of Things loves this word—
consider how porous it all is,
how there's always room
for atoms to do what they have their hearts set
on doing: finding windows
to slip in and out of, *secret passages,*
whole highways, pipes up our Roman troublemaker,
            in a thing that looked so solid
nothing could get through, doors flung open
where no doors seem possible.

Todd Davis

Biographical Statement

Todd Davis is the son of a veterinarian and a lay minister in the United Methodist Church. He has been married to Shelly Davis for the past eighteen years and has two sons, Noah and Nathan. He spends most of his time hiking and hunting the forests of the ridge and valley country of central Pennsylvania.

Todd Davis is the author of two poetry collections, *Ripe* (Bottom Dog Press, 2002) and *Some Heaven* (Michigan State University Press, 2006). He teaches at Penn State Altoona. His poems have appeared in such journals and magazines as *The North American Review*, *River Styx*, *Arts & Letters*, *Poetry East*, *Green Mountains Review*, *The Christian Science Monitor*, and *Image: A Journal of the Arts & Religion*, as well as in such anthologies as *A Cappella: Mennonite Voices in Poetry* (University of Iowa Press, 2003) and *Visiting Frost: Poems Inspired by the Life and Work of Robert Frost* (University of Iowa Press, 2005).

Tentative Gardening

I'm a tentative gardener. I love everything that lives, everything that grows. The lilacs I planted when we moved to this new house and whose strong blossoms fill the room as I write. The serviceberry tree whose flowers ran off with the wind more than a week ago and that now works hard to shape berries we will eat in June. The tiger lilies along the road whose green fingers broke the soil's veil the first week of March but whose bodies won't be fully exhumed until July when their orange flags will wave down any passing eye.

I say I'm a tentative gardener because death is always involved with the act of living. The rhododendron I planted several years ago died a slow death last fall, leaves turning brown, one by one, until only brittle limbs were left. The broccoli and cauliflower seedlings nipped this spring by an unexpected late frost. The hackberry, more than seventy years old, struck by lightening and sent withering into summer's drought.

I want to help things grow, but at times I'm afraid to. After all it's easy to see the spirit move in April and May's fecundity. Even in July and August, as long as the rains come when they're needed. But the greater challenge for me—as a father of two boys, as a husband and son, as a maker of poems—is to find spirit in the loss that threatens us. The war in Iraq. The predictions of a bird flu pandemic. The reality of the neighbor who lost a son to methadone addiction. And, of course, the far more mundane and ubiquitous ways we grow old and pass.

I suppose the first rule we all learn is that whatever grows must diminish. Thankfully, for me poems have been a book not only of consolation, but a memorial to resurrection and rebirth, to the cyclical nature of all living matter and its turning of itself into other living things.

Beyond any hope or faith in some metaphysical heaven—something I do profess as a Mennonite Christian—I'm assured of a new heaven and new earth right here everyday. Whenever I walk into the woods, whenever I feel the sun or moon upon my face, there is the sacred prayer of poetry. It's in the bones of a deer gnawed on by a porcupine; in the leaves of hickory and oak and ash as they dissolve and are remade into the red flower of wake-robin and the white of hepatica.

Resurrection is practiced all around us, even in the winter months when buds sleep, then slowly begin to build toward their ultimate opening. Too often we mistake gestation in the fields and forests as a time of death, of nothingness. Perhaps the death I perceive, that makes me a tentative gardener, is merely another kind of gestation, a dormancy that leads to a different kind of life, one that the spirit helps us to imagine.

As a writer I can only hope to be present to this spirit in each moment I'm given. To help myself, I often return to Emerson's proclamation that everything is a miracle, to Basho's wise admonition in his final poem that dreams wander on, and to Christ's proclamation that the kingdom is here, now, in this place.

Some Heaven

The rabbit's head is caught
between the slats of the fence,
and in its struggle it has turned
so the hind legs nearly touch
the nose—neck broken, lungs failing.
My boys ask me to do something
but see no mercy in my plan.
At four and seven, they are so far
away from their own deaths
that they cannot imagine the blessing
a shovel might hold, the lesson
suffering offers those who have
not suffered.

At bedtime, my youngest prays
the rabbit is in a heaven
where there are no fences, where
there is more than enough to eat.
He begins to cry and we rock
until sleep's embrace takes him
from me. I know his prayer is right.
What more should heaven be?
A place wild with carrot and dill,
sunflower and phlox, fields
that stretch on for miles, every coyote
full, every hawk passing over, a warm
October day that need never end.

Amish Gardens

For Elsie and David Kline

Toward the middle of September when late flowers
bloom and orange and red peppers dangle close

to chrysanthemums, the yellow squash and last zucchini
tangle, full hips writhing like new lovers caught

in pumpkin vines, the bold orange of their pregnant bellies
taking over everything. Here the order she worked hard

to cultivate through the unruly summer gives ground
to the growing season's final days, and she wonders

what might lurk under these large, green leaves; what exactly
was lost when we left the garden long ago. Little time

remains to tend to such matters, harvest hard upon her.
Yet she is bothered by the brightness of these last blossoms,

the way their mouths pout at the very thought of the first
hard frost—earth moist from melting cold, plow pushing it

all safely under, garden bed as dark and rich as her husband's
thighs hidden beneath plain trousers.

Prairie Liturgy

For Mary Swander
Only upon our failing breath may we speak.

I.

Words are carried
like small boats on the river
of our blood, oxygen dying
in the sails, hands braced
on gunwales.

II.

Without trust, we hold the first
word, then the next and the next
after—a stolen prayer, an early
moon half-eaten, plum bruised
and laid upon the horizon's table.

III.

When will the hornet's nest, nestled
in the branches of the locust, begin
to flutter, its gray lung turned pink?

IV.

Fox and deer hide in the prairie's last
remnant, concealed by the ravines that fall
away like creases in the brain or the ridges
of a hedge apple, florid green and hard
as stone.

V.

What evidence of the bobcat? Only her kill—
tracks circled, hind paws leaping, a bird's
downy plume laid at the bottom of the creek
where water freezes come November and snow,
like a shroud, veils all until April.

VI.

A highway runs
where the ocean once lay,
and here winds blow for days,
birthed upon a sea, borne
up over mountains to the flat,
open space of this field.

VII.

The red-tailed hawk cares nothing
for judgment, sees no good or bad
as it sits on a mile-marker, waiting out
passing cars to dine on what we kill.

VIII.

We cannot hold
our breath
forever—in time
this prayer
will slip
from us.

IX.

Today the grasses rise and fall, as they do
at sea. And this bird's wing-beat helps
move the stems, takes the seed and delivers
it into the earth where the sun will drag it
toward heaven, all of our heads bowed
and bent by the wind.

X.

What else is there but supplication?
Bee dips into flower's bowl, bobcat's belly
full, small polished bones in the osprey's
nest, and scat of all kinds spread beneath
the basswood in honor of the lives taken.

XI.

On the plain that rises beyond the river,
September grasses begin to fire, smoke
visible for miles, great curtains of flame
opening and closing, telling a story
of a world without end.

XII.

Amen.

Prayer Requests at a Mennonite Church

Pray for the Smucker family. Their son Nathaniel's coat and shirt were caught in the gears while grinding grain. Nothing would give, so now he is gone. We made his clothes too well. Perhaps this is our sin.

Pray for the Birky family. Their son Jacob fell to his death in the granary. He was covered in corn before they could stop the pouring—chest crushed by the weight, seed spilling from his mouth. We hope something will grow from this, besides our grief.

Pray for the Hartzler family. Their youngest has left the church and no longer believes that Christ died for her sins. She buys clothes at the mall. Tongue pierced, nose as well. Her shirt shows her belly where a ring of gold sprouts. We pray she will remember that her Lord's side was pierced, that his crown held no gold, only the dried blood of his brow.

Pray for the Miller family. Last week their daughter, who lives in Kalona, lost her baby at birth. Child only half-formed: head turned the wrong way; heart laid on the outside of her chest; one leg little more than an afterthought. Lord, help them know that life may come again, that we are all made whole in heaven.

Pray for the Stutzman family. Their son fights in the war. We call him back to the Prince of Peace, to our Savior who knelt to gather the slave's ear, brushed the dirt away, lifted it to the side of his flushed face. May we leave no scars. May we ask no blessing for the killing done in His name.

How Else

would God enter this room except through curtains
of light, muslin sliding over your hip as you lie
on your side? And what of the leaves beyond
the window pane that turn first to the sun, then back,
as if invisible hands held the course each must take?
What more evidence might we wish for to believe

that certain spirits travel from east to west? Surely
this late moon that hangs against the color of the coming
day, a blue that will fade before noon, holds everything

we will never understand.

Travis Wayne Denton

Biographical Statement

Travis Wayne Denton was born in Rome, Georgia, and moved around quite a bit as a child before settling down in Cedartown, Georgia, just south of Rome. He ended up marrying his pastor's daughter, Caron. He now lives in Atlanta where he is the Editor of *Terminus Magazine*, an international magazine of the arts, and he is the Associate Director of Poetry at Tech, a program at Georgia Tech which has brought poetry and creative writing to Georgia Tech, along with offering a reading series and workshops for the community. His work has appeared or is forthcoming in journals such as *Greensboro Review*, *Rattle, South Carolina Review*, and many others.

Statement:

Spirituality has always played a central role in my poetry and the reason for that is because Christianity has always played such a role in my life. As a child, I moved quite a bit because of my father's job and in each town we moved to, one of the first things we had to do was to find a home, then a church and these churches were not always the same denomination as the one before. As a child, I was everything from a Seventh Day Adventist to Baptist, before finally settling on the Assemblies of God. So I was able to view the religious landscape on a number of different levels, but although there were many differences in the denominations and oftentimes they spoke poorly of one another, the one common thread was belief in God and the fact that no matter how bad things got down here with sickness or war or anything else, there was always the promise of "a better place" waiting and that was comforting to me from a young age. I enjoyed knowing that each of us would someday "Leave the Body Behind." I was always fascinated with this idea of perfect freedom without having the body to weigh us down. So from that idea grew the idea for my latest manuscript, where most of these poems will appear, which is called "Leaving the Body Behind."

As my poetic sensibility continued to develop, I felt more of a need to understand exactly why, in my poetry, I deal so much with spirituality and what I've come to understand over the years is that I believe poetry and spirituality come from similar places within the human psyche. As humans, most of us have some sort of an intuitive need to connect with a force or something greater than the self. We want to believe in a "magic" of sorts. It makes us feel better to put things in someone else's hands when life gets tough. For the poet, the work of "making" or creating art is also a way of achieving that feeling of connection. It is a way of connecting the dots, so to speak. It is a way of pulling together all these seemingly unconnected images, and putting them all on the page in hopes of creating something that is beautiful and meaningful which not only serves to soothe the soul of the poet, but if the poet has done his job right, others will connect with the work and for a while share in that feeling of beauty or connection.

Some say I'm lucky,
the way I lived through my death

but there are many of us who have refused
to be spirited out the world, only to be
coaxed down a long hallway holding a warm hand
and not saying a word. And consider those
who simply floated out of themselves for a time,
rising
above the operating table
as the doctors
and nurses all sighed and took a step back.

But my would-be death wasn't as interesting
as those I've read about or seen on TV:
I never saw my life flash in front of me,
no quick review of my utter triumphs and failures—
I didn't feel the wind
give me a gentle push from behind
as I stood on the rim of a great canyon

watching falcons spiral into the red and purple hues
of the desert sundown, nor did I hear
my name mispronounced at a graduation,
or think of my last cigarette.

But when my breath finally left me
after the airbag's sudden punch
and I thought, "so this is how it ends"
as I looked for that cliché of light that swirls
around you like your mother wrapping
you in a blanket after a warm bath,
I gritted my teeth and opened my eyes
in a doll-like stare and I saw
that broken windshield, and through it,
a barn flower, just across the highway,
and heard the voices of the living
calling me back
to all the odd particulars of this world.

Returning the Indian Pottery

Is it the Indian Pottery that did it all: set these two years
of woes into motion: made a once good right foot go sour,
the bills, and oh yes, the legal trouble?

We didn't see the signs along the canyon trail:
the warnings of impending doom, nor did we hear
the stories of warrior spirits hitching rides in Samsonite,
following grinning tourists with their relics home

in their Beamers and Sport Utes, waiting for the right time
to sprinkle their bad mojo and reclaim kin.

It was there in the grass, just off the trail at Bandalier,
a short walk through the canyon and past
the longhouses, the Anasazi condos, on the way
to the great ceremonial kiva.

Just a few pieces of broken clay, perhaps a water jug,

a cooker, a piss pot, sealed with pitch and painted
with ash and deer blood. It doesn't suit
the coffee table anymore. It never made a centerpiece—

not like the family Bible. But I'm not superstitious.
I step on cracks, walk under ladders. I saw my wife
before the wedding. A string of bad luck, that's all.
A down-cycle. Happens all the time.

If it helps, take it back, oh great Indian god of rain,
god of fire, god of pine nuts.
It's in the mail.

Porter Got Ahead of the Lord

He'd taken up snakes before. He liked rattlers:
the way diamondbacks would wrap themselves
around his wrist and look him straight in the eye.

When he heard that steady two/four on the drums
and the twang of Bobby's guitar, he felt the spirit move.
He'd dance a shuffle and reach into that dark wood box.

But it was Independence Day when Porter got ahead of the Lord.
He moved before the spirit did. He took the biggest
of the bunch above his head and that's when it stung him.

The crowd gasped, but the band played on.
The room, full of sweaty bodies, spun in time as Porter
laid back on the pew and Tom bashed the devil-snake with his boot.

He felt the Holy Ghost screaming through his veins like whiskey.
Porter what do you feel? I see angels across the river
in Beulahland and mamma standing in the light.

There were sirens and a laying-on of hands. He lay there
shouting *Save Me Baby Save Me,* and foaming at the mouth
as the preacher waved the paramedics away

and Porter shivered once, then closed his eyes.

Camille Dungy

Biographical Statement

Camille Dungy is the daughter of a preacher's kid and, therefore, spent most summers of her youth attending strangers' weddings, funerals and baptisms. She has attended countless receptions hosted by people she does not really know, and she's eaten a lot of cake in church basements. To this day, Dungy is not afraid of to go to other people's parties, and she maintains a fondness for church basements.

Camille Dungy author of *What to Eat, What to Drink, and What to Leave for Poison* (Red Hen Press 2006), has received fellowships and awards from organizations including the National Endowment for the Arts, The Virginia Commission for the Arts, Cave Canem, The American Antiquarian Society, and the Bread Loaf Writer's Conference. She is associate editor of *Gathering Ground: A Reader Celebrating Cave Canem's First Decade.* Dungy currently lives in San Francisco, California where she serves as Associate Professor in the Creative Writing Department at San Francisco State University.

Statement:

When I was sixteen, I nearly came to Jesus. We were visiting family in Pine Bluff, Arkansas, and that Sunday Cousin James Lenzie preached a sermon that made me want to jump up and shout.

Religious talk runs in my family the way alcoholism runs in others.' The way a patriarch might pass his drinking habit on to his sons and nephews, his daughters, his wife's sister's eldest son, preaching and praying afflicts the generations in my clan. In some homes families gather around a table, dish out rum-soaked sweet potatoes and pour out bottle after bottle of bourbon, beer, or wine. In mine, we pour over scriptural interpretations of the bodily resurrection of Christ, dish out advice on how to fill the Mainline Protestant church's fast-emptying pews. My people talk about Biblical characters as if they're folks they know, as if Mary and Martha or Isaac or Cain might just sit down and join us for supper sometime. My people often leave a chair free for Elijah.

I was sixteen and twice baptized (the infant anti-calamity model and the quincaeñera/confirmation kind). I'd spent most every Sunday of my life in church, and quite a few Saturday afternoons and Wednesday evenings too. My grandfather's a Baptist minister and, as I visited him nearly every summer of my life, I'd spent nearly every summer of my life eating, sleeping, dressing, playing, dreaming, praying, flirting, sneezing, laughing, reading, running, sitting, living in his church. I was no newcomer to the idea that religion could be part of my everyday life, but in his sermon my cousin recalled to me a face of God I hadn't known I'd missed.

Still, I did not walk to the front of the church that day when he invited me to come to Jesus. This was because I quickly realized my ardor might have had less to do with God than with my excitement over what language can do for our understanding of and relationship to whatever it is we identify as God. The basic gist of my cousin's sermon presented something my family and I assumed I'd accepted long ago, but the actual words he used and the arrangement in which he presented them this Sunday suggested something different, something new.

My grandfather says a good sermon should evoke. According to my computer's *Oxford American Dictionary*, evoke is a transitive verb meaning to "bring or recall to the conscious mind," to "elicit a response," or to "invoke (a spirit or deity)." I have no recollection of what my cousin preached about that day and, for this story, the particulars hardly matter. What matters is that James Lenzie's sermon had given a form, for a moment, to the kinetic air (call it God if you will), had given word to things I'd felt but never named before. If sermons are an art form (and why not?) James Lenzie's had achieved what I believe to be one of the highest aims of art: he provided a form for the previously formless and then it was as if it could never have not possessed that form before.

What had made me want to jump up and shout in James Lenzie's sermon is the same sort of thing that makes me want to jump up and shout when I read a great line of poetry or a masterfully inventive turn of phrase, when I think about the zipper or safety matches and how they changed the world, when I see Calder's mobiles, hear Coltrane's "My Favorite Things"; I'm thrilled whenever I encounter a creation that embodies an inevitable surprise. The beauty in these creations comes largely from the fact that the invention (of language, of structure, of concept), once revealed, is shocking in its obviousness, its correctness. Why had no one ever thought to formulate things quite that way before?

What had made me want to jump up and shout in James Lenzie's sermon was the way he revealed a portal for transcendence in my day-to-day life. He just zipped something open, struck a match and let me see by it's light. That's what I think of when I think of the spiritual aspects of art (my cousin's sermon, my own poetry, Beethoven's 5th, any art). I'm interested in the portals toward greater understanding or experience that are opened or illuminated through art.

Some months ago I joined a church. After more than fifteen years without a regular affiliation, I got up one Sunday, put on my best pants and a smart pair of shoes, drove to church, and at the end of the service I did what I had not done for James Lenzie, answered the minister's invitation and walked to the altar.

I still suspect this might have had little to do with God and more to do with the language this particular congregation used to approach the Spirit.

The first Sunday I visited this church I knew it was a church for me. Mostly because they quoted Gerard Manley Hopkins on the bulletin and also because the minister referred to an Adrienne Rich poem during the course of his sermon. This Easter, even after I explained to the minister that I thought Easter was largely an appropriate agricultural festival and fertility rite, they let me read a crown of sonnets about how spring in Virginia makes me ecstatic. And when I say ecstatic I mean that in my dictionary's "involving an experience of mystic self-transcendence" kind of way. I suspect my ardor for this particular congregation had something to do with their respect for the different ways humans aspire to make the unseen seen and their willingness to seek language for the things behind the things we see. I suspect I liked this particular crowd of Christians partly because they believed that poetry is a viable means through which we might construct a language of illumination.

"The thing I think your poetry does," said my fellow congregant, Jack Scudder, "is disclose the spiritual in the lived world. Not the world considered as object, but the world in which we live." The example he gave was not one of my poems that allude to religious figures, nor one that speaks directly of my grandfather, the preacher man. The poem he mentioned was one about a young man dancing with a woman and learning from that something about physical love. A potential portal for transcendence that kind of love is, certainly.

I didn't walk up the aisle when my cousin James Lenzie invited me because I remember thinking I already felt something powerful moving through and all around me, and though his sermon named it in a way that thrilled me because it was at once so foreign and familiar, it was not, in the end, a formulation I was prepared to claim. Though his sermon gave the buzz I felt around me one name, I knew I would, some way, some day, have to choose my own word(s).

What made me want to jump up and shout was less what my cousin actually said all those years ago than it was my excitement at his construction of language, a thrill at the fact that the world as I knew it could be so startlingly and yet obviously observed and thusly rearranged. Though I would stand up and move around inside language eventually, though I would even commit myself to communities dedicated to processing the word, that day I sat still. I kept my place in the family pew and thought about how I might, one day, make language zing in that same ecstatic, holy, original, inexorable way.

Service Station, Tennessee

Even a man of God sometimes runs out
of prayers. But with his pretty wife and girls
there with him, all their bodies locked inside
that loose-rod car, Thornton couldn't think that
he might meet silence soon.
                                        There was no one
who would help. Only six men hammering
their palms with wrenches, fixing other cars,
saying, *We'll get to you when we're through here.*

Then a kid on furlough from Korea,
where his own life was watched by Negro men,
tailed their car to Knoxville.

                                        There was no choice.
The soldier warned him, *These are my people.*
Man, I know them. If you can move this car
at all, leave this town. Leave while you still can.

My Grandmother Takes the Youth Group to Services

The sky's wide open blue told her, *Go in*
where you have never been before, and where
she went she took the children. Older girls
in long skirts, little black heels, white collars
rough with starch, and hair still hot from the comb,
along with boys their age, pants creased, shoes blacked
and bright. Little Linda in Topeka
had upset no one yet, but that black shock,
Lynchburg's largest high school class in years, did.

Surprised, the white minister welcomed her

with silence, but that evening his voice fumed
through Thornton's phone. *Your pretty wife should trust*
the good Lord's plan. Let her know, in heaven,
negroes will have to learn their rightful place.

Ark

I will enter you as hope enters me,
through blinding liquid, light of rain, and I
will stay inside until you send me out;
I will stay inside until you ground me.
We cannot outrun the rain. So many
summers I have tried. So many summers.
But when the rumble calls after the spark
there can be no escape. No outstripping
the drench soak, the wet sheath, the water caul.
This is more than you want to hear. Much more
than I want to tell you. Tabernacle
transporting my life from the desert, you,
the faith I am born and reborn into,
you, rescuer, deliverer of rain.

and thou shalt be called a new name

which the mouth of the Lord shall name

***

For Zion's sake I will not
I will not hold my peace

For Jerusalem's sake I will not

I will not rest   I will not
I will not rest until the righteous go

***

it was the roaming creature's birthright she was after
so she marked the wanderings of a sick buck till it died
it was the wild creature's right to free death she desired

***

the righteous go forth
as the brightness the brightness

the righteous go forth as the brightness and the salvation thereof

as the lamps that burneth

***

she marked the failing of a sick buck when it died
then stowed her traveling dress beneath the carcass

in three days she'd made a stench skirt to slow the hounds
still more
she polished her boots in his hide's rot
sweet oil

***

and the Gentiles shall see the Gentiles shall
the Gentiles shall see thy righteousness and all the kings shall see thy glory

***

she named herself Rebecca because that woman knew
smell could run privilege out of a brute's tent
and secure it for the child she favored

***

Thou shalt no more be called Forsaken
neither shall thy land be termed Desolate

***

she was awhile preparing

but when she smelled most like disappearing
she was gone

Sunday Morning

Desire swung like that: like her
legs in procession, like perfume
from a censer on its linked chain.
Heavy as smoke in the hold's light,
desire. A church, a cathedral, the body
in that robe. The robe sash swinging.
The progress through the sinning body
to this sacred spot. A man kneeling.
A man with head bent. A man lifting
his prayer to a woman. Desire. Desire. Desire.
                                        Grant us grace.

Annunciation

Perhaps in the peace of her dreams
her skin is the skin of unharvested fruit. Flesh not worth

thorns. Perhaps she dreams no sparrow,
no lark's beak, no clasped and unclasped hands will seek her, withered,

wrinkled as she is. In truth, she has lived through the dying
of men children and virgin hope, but she has never been

an old woman. Never anything but young. Like the queen
whose body is renewed each day in someone else's blood,

as if suffering were the secret source of youth. She wakes
and understands the passion cries that draw her young body

are nothing but the high sounds of her name. Year after year
Mary will remain just the girl

we expect. All through the ages she'll remain. The girl with
only one dream worth repeating.

Stephen Dunn

Biographical Statement

Stephen Dunn: I was born in Forest Hills, New York in 1939. My parents and my brother and I lived with my maternal grandparents, a German Jew and a Scotch Protestant. My father was an Irish Catholic, and my mother, somewhat hesitantly, converted to Catholicism. I was brought up as a Catholic, but around our dinner table no orthodoxy was possible. I now live in western Maryland, with my wife, the writer Barbara Hurd.

Stephen Dunn is the author of fourteen collections of poetry, the most recent of which is *Everything Else in the World.* His *Different Hours* won the 2001 Pulitzer Prize.

Another World

As an atheist and skeptic, I've long held dear Paul Eluard's statement, "There is another world, and it is in this one." It has been my credo as a poet. I take it as a given that my job is to enact and deliver both worlds, which involves giving voice to interiorities and evanescences, and to the surfaces that conceal and evoke them. I try to say what's difficult to say, the elusive things we feel but are inarticulate about. Such utterances, formed and framed, make forays into what, for me, is the spiritual world. Nevertheless, I remain fascinated by the idea of God, and the cross-cultural, sacred texts that embody this insistent idea, and the collective psychology that can be inferred from them.

Religion

First, it was more about mystery than about trying to get us to behave. Whichever, we're still in some lonely cave, not far from that moment a lightning storm or a sunset drove us to invent the upper reaches of the sky. Religion is proof that a good story, well-told, is a powerful thing. Proof, too, that terror makes fabulists of us all. We're pitiful, finally, and so oddly valiant. The dead god rising into ism after ism—that longing for coherence that keeps us, if not naïve, historically challenged. To love Christ you must love the Buddha, to love Mohammed or Moses you must love Confucius and, say, Schopenhauer and Nietzsche as well. They were all wise and unsponsored and insufficient, some of the best of us. I'm saying this to myself: the sacred cannot be found unless you give up some old version of it. And when you do, *mon semblable, mon frère*, I swear there'll be an emptiness it'll take a lifetime to fill. Indulge, become capacious, give up nothing, Jack my corner grocer said. He was pushing the portobellos, but I was listening with that other, my neediest ear.

Scapegoat

It's the Day of Atonement, and Aaron has a brilliant idea. Two goats as offerings to the Lord. One he kills as a personal atonement for himself and his house. The other is the scapegoat. He lays both hands on its head, confessing the sins of the people, then sends it off into the wilderness. Poor goats. Lucky, unburdened people. It's easy to see why such an idea caught on. There's a burnt offering too, involving a ram; in the face of the ineffable, Aaron tries to cover all bases. But we're most interested in the goat that bears our large and small mistakes, and carries them away from us. Leviticus knew how to tell a story, but here's what was never reported: The Lord saw the goat in the wilderness, stumbling, half-dead. He said to it: A goat's life is an awful thing. This was not My intention. What they've done to you is just one more of their sins.

Knowledge

Some things like stones yield
only their opacity,
remain inscrutably themselves.
To the trained eye they offer their age,
some small planetary news.

Which suggests the world
becomes more mysterious, not less,
the more we know.

God knows is how we begin a sentence
when we refuse to acknowledge what we know.

Gravitas is what Newton must have felt
when gravity became clear to him.

Presto, said the clown as he pulled
a quarter from behind my ear
when I was five. The very same ear in fact
that pressed itself to a snail's vacant house
and found an ocean.

The problem is how to look intelligent
with our mouths agape,
how to be delighted, not stupefied
when the caterpillar shrugs
and becomes a butterfly.

It takes a clear surface
to properly lead us into mystery.

God knows nothing we don't know.
We gave him every word he ever said.

Here

Maybe this world
is another planet's Hell.
– Aldous Huxley

Sometimes it feels otherworldly, what I've felt,
my heart residing in its own peculiar dark,
or suddenly aglow, lit up from within.
I sense then I'm on one of the good planets

where mistakes and wild, venal joys
lead to ordinary suffering, not banishment or doom.
                    Whatever we must endure,
doesn't it take place closer to home?

I know how I feel about murderers or men
with lollipops who lead children into the woods.
Still, eternal damnation doesn't do
anyone any good. Most of us pay now

for what we do and have done, or slide
like the poor and the helpless toward
the slammed gavel of a fate. That's enough, I say
out loud to no one in any world. Yet here

          and there, though mostly here, even fate is reversible
with struggle or luck. More than once I've walked
under the sun and beneath the luminous moon
not knowing what or whom to thank.

The Death of God

When the news filtered to the angels
they were overwhelmed by their sudden aloneness.
Long into the night they waited for instructions;
the night was quieter than any night they'd known.
I don't have a thought in my head, one angel lamented.
Others worried, Is there such a thing as an angel now?

New to questioning, dashed by the dry light
of reason, some fell into despair. Many disappeared.
A few wandered naturally toward power, were hired
by dictators who needed something like an angel
to represent them to the world.
These angels spoke the pure secular word.
They murdered sweetly and extolled the greater good.
The Dark Angel himself was simply amused.

The void grew, and was fabulously filled.
Vast stadiums and elaborate malls—
the new cathedrals—were built
where people cheered and consumed.
At the nostalgia shops angel trinkets
and plastic crucifixes lined the shelves.
The old churches were homes for the poor.
And yet before meals and at bedtime
and in the iconographies of dreams,
God took his invisible place in the kingdom of need.
Disaffected minstrels made and sang His songs.
The angels were given breath and brain.
This all went on while He was dead to the world.

The Dark Angel observed it, waiting as ever.
On these things his entire existence depended.

Afterlife

There've been times I've thought worms
    might be beneficent, speeding up,
as they do, the dissolution of the body.

I've imagined myself streamlined, all bone
    and severity,
pure mind, free to contemplate the startling

absence of any useful metaphysics, any final
    punishment or reward.
Indulgences, no doubt. Romances I've allowed myself

when nothing ached, and the long diminishment
    seemed far off.
Today I want my body to keep making its sloppy

requests. I'm out among the wayward dazzle
    of the countryside,
which is its own afterlife, wild, repeatable.

There's no lesson in it for me. I just like
    its ignorant thrust,
it's sure way back, after months without desire.

Are wildflowers holy? Are weeds?
    There's infinite hope
if both are, but perhaps not for us.

To skirt the woods, to walk deeply like this
    into the high grass,
is to invoke the phantasms of sense

and importance. I think I'm smelling the rain
    we can smell before it rains.
It's the odor of another world, I'm convinced,

and means nothing, yet here it is, and here
    sweetly it comes
from the gray sky into the small openings.

Salvation

Finally, I gave up on obeisance,
and refused to welcome
either retribution or the tease

of sunny days. As for the can't-be-
seen, the sum-of-all-details,
the One—oh when it came

to salvation I was only sure
I needed to be spared
someone else's version of it.

The small prayers I devised
had in them the hard sounds
of *split* and *frost*.

In the beaconless dark
I wanted them to speak
as if it made sense to speak

to what isn't there.
I wanted them to startle
by how little they asked.

Stuart Dybek

Biographical Sketch

Stuart Dybeck lives in Kalamazoo, Michigan, where he teaches at Western Michigan University. As a youth he worked at labor jobs in construction, washed helicopters, painted buildings, hired out for Man Power day labor. He also worked as a bookkeeper, copywriter, and caseworker for Cook County Department of Public Aid.

Stuart Dybek is the author of two collections of poetry: *Streets in Their Own Ink* (FSG) and *Brass Knuckles* (Carnegie Mellon.) He has also written three books of fiction. He is Distinguished Writer in Residence at Northwestern University and a member of the permanent faculty in the Prague Summer Program.

Spiritual Dimensions

The spiritual dimension in my work often arises from the cultural context that naturally arises when sense of place is a central element. All these poems are set in a working class, immigrant neighborhood on Chicago's South Side. The neighborhood's main ethnic groups are Mexican and Polish, cultures that are traditionally Catholic. The highest peaks in this neighborhood are still the spires of its many churches. In such a setting, spirituality serves as a counterpoint to the tough, and sometimes brutal, realities of assimilation, prejudice, and poverty. To convey the spiritual, religion afford a vocabulary of the sacred and of awe. It is a vocabulary a poem can employ even when the subject is not so much belief or faith, but rather, mystery.

Confession

Father Boguslaw was the priest I waited for, the one whose breath through the thin partition of the confessional reminded me of the ventilator behind Vic's Tap. He huffed and smacked as if in response to my dull litany of sins, and I pictured him slouched in his cubicle, draped in vestments, the way he sat slumped in the back entrance to the sacristy before saying morning mass—hung over, sucking an unlit Pall Mall, exhaling smoke.

Once, his head thudded against the wooden box.

"Father," I whispered, "Father," but he was out, snoring. I knelt wondering what to do, until he finally groaned and hacked himself awake.

As usual, I'd saved the deadly sins for last: the lies and copied homework, snitching drinks, ditching school, hitchhiking, which I'd been convinced was an offense against the Fifth Commandment, which prohibited suicide. Before I reached the dirty snapshots of Korean girls, stolen from the dresser of my war hero uncle, Uncle Al, and still unrepentantly cached behind the oil shed, he knocked and said I was forgiven.

As for Penance: "Go in peace, my son, I'm suffering enough today for both of us."

Benediction

The fly is giving another sermon;
we bow to mud, receiving absolution from a worm.
Impatient with the pace of prayer
—the journey's too long to make on our knees—
we scour the alleys for discarded slogans,
for proverbs banned from Bibles,
ignited by guitars—electric fire
branding air with a graffiti of psalms.

My clothesline whip drove wind and stars;
pigeons, not ponies, pulled my droshky,
At dusk, we traced the peddler's dirge
to the misted mouth
of a viaduct that swallowed full moons.
The horizon was strung on the other side,
But when a border of boxcars rumbled its drums
we fled down the neon tail

of the comet known as Cermak Road.
Night was that narrow—
a strip of darkness between shop signs.
Snow fell from the height
of a streetlamp.
I knew the names of seven attending angels
But was seventeen before I saw
my first jay.

Yet I worshipped the natural world
Like an immigrant
in an adopted country—
the one in which he should have been born.
For me, the complexity of a grasshopper
catapulting
from the Congo behind a billboard
was irrefutable proof
of God and his baffling order.
And in my heart
I still kneel on a weed lot in summer,
seeking benedication
beneath the glittering cross
of a dragonfly.

Gwiajtska*

Beneath a star that burns in snowing skies,
The pilot light, blue as baby's eyes,
bows to a draft that might be the wake
of spirits feeling through the dark.

Don't make a wish when it blows out—
it's not *your* birthday. Don't kneel
before the oven door left open for heat—
you're not with Busha in a barn that smells

of incense rather than farm animals
huddled by racks of guttering vigil candles.
Don't offer coins that Jesus knows you stole

from blind, old Novak's open till.

Hasn't the Good Book taught you not to pray
before a fire that can't sear meat?

**A Polish word for Christmas Even, meaning Christmas Star.*

Angelus

It's the metallic hour
When birds lose perfect pitch.
On a porch, three stories up,
against the copper window
facing the El,
a woman in a satin slip
and the geraniums she waters
turn to gold.

Beneath the street the blue clapper
of a switch swings in the tunnel.
Blocks away, a crescendo is overtaken
By its echo, and the reverberation
passes among strangers.
Shadows quiver like sheet metal.
High heels pace off down a platform
like one hand on a piano.

There's a note struck every evening—
every evening held longer—
a clang only because it's surrounded by silence,
chimes of small change
from the newsstand, trousers
full of keys and coins
flopped on a chair beside the bed,
the tink of bracelets
as her arm sweeps back her hair.

Halo

Read the Braille of worn wallpaper, decode
the remains of symbols on a threadbare carpet:
a design nights of pacing leave behind
leading to a hidden space that smells of childhood,
a darkened flat of cross words that can't be taken back,
a kitchen of chopped carrots and snapped beans,
where the fingerprint of worry is the coil of a hot plate,
and memory rumbles to the boil of water.
At the end of a hall that grows ever longer,
a living room ghostly in the sour, milky film
of a chandelier of cataracts. Father,
face hidden, work clothes smoldering
from the night shift at the foundry, leans
his forehead against the cold, steamed window,
unconscious of your presence, as you've been
unconscious of his absence, until this moment,
when you've seen grace reflected in the gleam
around the tonsure of his bald spot.

Penance

It was always Good Friday
Those Saturday afternoons.
Stooped babkas in black coats
and babushkas, kneeling
in marble aisles
before racks of vigil candles,
faces buried in hands.
Weeping echoes through the dim church
As foreign as their droned
language of prayer.
I stood in line
waiting the priest's question,
"Alone or with others?"
and my turn in Confession,

trying to imagine
the terrible sins of old women.

Stain

Snow was falling last night when I returned
to my parish church. Without the snow
I couldn't have traced my old boot prints,
nor would the blood have been easy to follow,
trailed as if someone staggering home from the dentist,
with a handkerchief pressed to his mouth, paused
every few steps to spit out the taste of metal.
Dulled by cold, bells hammered an hour out of tune
with the times. As if the daily concussion
of chimes had eroded stone, the neighborhood
below the steeple stood devastated—
windows blown, walls supported by graffiti,
backyards reduced to plots of graves.
The waifs, winos, and petty hoods
who once were local heroes, were wanted now
for crimes against humanity.
Somewhere in hiding the President prayed,
but here a stain was soaking through snow
as if wounds on bodies half-buried in frozen earth
were leaking through gauze, a stain
visible in every exhaled breath and in the fog
fuming from sewers, and the exhausts of limousines
that idled beneath the blink of bar signs,
and the slick of brake lights on black ice.
Before the embers of bankrupt foundries,
the rusty river flowed like an opened vein.

Angie Estes

Biographical Sketch

Angie Estes: My early years were spent on the East Coast, in Maryland and Virginia, where we had lightning bugs every summer. Both sides of my family came from Virginia, and my mother's family lived—no one could remember how long—in the Blue Ridge Mountains until they were moved out when their land was taken to become part of Shenandoah National Park. I was raised as a Southern Baptist. Now I live in Ohio, where we have lightning bugs every summer.

Angie Estes' most recent book is *Chez Nous* (Oberlin College Press, 2005). Her second book, *Voice-Over* (2002), won the *FIELD* Poetry Prize and the Alice Fay di Castagnola Prize from the Poetry Society of America. Her first book, *The Uses of Passion* (1995), received the Peregrine Smith Poetry Prize.

Stained Glass Spirituality

The twelfth-century Abbot of St. Denis, Suger, wrote of how his delight in and meditation on the beautiful objects of the material world produced an instantaneous, joyous transport to a "higher world": "Thus, when—out of my delight in the beauty of the house of God—the loveliness of the many-coloured gems has called me away from external cares, and worthy meditation has induced me to reflect, transferring that which is material to that which is immaterial, on the diversity of the sacred virtues: then it seems to me that I see myself dwelling, as it were, in some strange region of the universe which neither exists entirely in the slime of the earth nor entirely in the purity of Heaven…."

A poem—with its arrangement of the beautiful and strange hieroglyphs of the world—like a massive stained-glass rose window, transforms what passes through it and enables us to dwell for a moment in that "strange region of the universe."

True Confessions

If I'd been a ranch, they would've
called me the Bar Nothing.
from *Gilda,* 1946

I can never get a zipper
to close. Maybe that stands
for something, what do you think?
I think glamour is its own
allure, thrashing and
flashing, a lure, a spoon
as in spooning, as in *l'amour*
in Scotland, where I once watched
the gorse-twisted hills unzip
to let a cold blue lake
between them. St. Augustine says
the reason why humans behave
as they do is because they are
not living in their true
home. In Rita Hayworth's
first film, for example, *Dante's Inferno*
is a failing Coney Island
concession, and Margarita Cansino
plays the part of Rita
Cansino playing herself. And the true
home of glamour, by which
I mean of course the grammar
of glamour, is Scotland
because *glamour* is a Scottish variant
of *grammar* with its rustle of moods
and desires. Which brings us back to
the zipper and why we want it
to close, each hook climbing another
the way words ascend a sentence, trying on
its silver suture like clothes. In a satin
strapless gown, Gilda slowly peeled off
her black arm-length gloves, showed
how to strip down, diagram a sentence: *Put*
the blame on Mame, boys. In 1946, a pin-up
of Rita Hayworth and the name *Gilda*

rode on the side of the atomic bomb
tested at Bikini Atoll; it was summer
and you could buy a record, hear the sound
of her beating heart. By her last
film, *The Wrath of God*, her hair was a burning
bush; she couldn't remember
her lines, whether it's memory or loss
we're in need of most: to remember
the way home or forget
who we are when we get there.
Every man I have known has fallen
in love with Gilda and wakened
with me. St. Augustine asked, *But when I love you,*
what do I love? He asked the earth
and the breeze, perfume, song,
flesh, the sun, the moon
and stars: *My question was the attention*
I gave to them, and their response
was their beauty.

Proverbs

Mortise and tenon, tongue and
groove, tongue-in-cheek, the tenor
holds the note until it dovetails
in air like the white kerchief of
the Holy Spirit tied around the neck
of God in Masaccio's *Trinity*, the dove
more banner than bird, which from
the beginning was the word for
verb—part sky, part earth, part
of speech expressing action, occurrence,
existence. *It is wonderful,*
Stein said, *the number of mistakes*
a verb can make. Pardon, scusi, word
for word, tell me whether the theory
holds and, if so, how we will
hold up, hold out, hold
on, and then I will hold you

to your promise the way the arms of God
hold up the cross, which holds up
Christ. *To have and to hold*: hold
that thought. *Besides being able to be*
mistaken and to make mistakes
verbs can change to look like
themselves or to look
like something else. The inscription above
the skeleton below Christ's feet, for example,
says the same holds
for you: *I was that which you are,*
and what I am you will be. So much
for *vers libre*. *Do you think he looks*
like himself? they asked, glancing toward
his casket. *In the hold*, in Masaccio's fresco,
the grave is a wall with a barrel vault
pierced through, deep chamber below
a coffered ceiling where God holds forth
in rose and black. *Behold,*
I show you a mystery: a ruse
is a ruse is a ruse. In Latin,
to have verve is to have
words. It could be a version,
aversion, a verse: please
advise. Not much we can know save
the redbud, which wears its heart
on its leaves.

Chapel

Scabbard *sans* dagger;
sheath or hooded cape, shrine
of hanging shoots that eventually find
the ground and root, tightening
trunks around a tree they never
mention. They worship that way
for centuries until rot leaves
only architecture's gesture
of embrace, reliquary

with no trace of a relic.
                    Who first imagined
the banyan—all gape and token—God's idea
of topiary, everything clipped in the shape
of nothing. Built in the thirteenth century,
Sainte Chapelle—its walls made of nothing
but light—was designed to hold
holy relics of the passion
of Christ: the Crown of Thorns, a piece of the True
Cross, fragments of the Holy Lance, Holy
Sponge, Christ's Mantel and Shroud, the Precious
Blood, and the Milk and Hair
of the Virgin. *One of the most beautiful residences of*
paradise, a fourteenth-century theologian called it.
          Flamboyant ribs,
highly elaborate, embellished, ornate—*flamboyer*, to blaze—
and why not? The light stayed on
while the relics went out, and the chapel
turned into *topos* incarnate, the body
of place. It's where we want
to be: *Like no place on earth,*
is what we say, as the rose roulette window
revolves overhead and we stumble
inside, a pair of dice.
                    Medieval saints placed all bets
on light they could hold like Bordeaux in a glass, called
it fair, made it bear the weight
of stone. They believed
the Persians when they said
hedge your bets, *pairi-daeza*, put a wall
around anything you might want
to keep. The caul and the body, apricot glaze
over *tarte aux pommes*: such a thin layer
between stone and hope, the violet nave
and air. From *someplace*,
                         maybe *the* place, saints gaze
through veined windows, like *sommeliers*, and nod
their advice: say *banyan*, say
snake eyes, say *building*, say *wall*;
say *chapel*, *c'est lips* that give shape

to whatever comes
between them, enclose
open space, make pleasure
spoken.

Rendez-vous

after Bernini

She's the *crème de la crème, la crème*
de God's *coeur*, pure
as butter under the painted sky,
and He, the light falling always
from an unseen source, narrowing
in gilded shafts to pierce
her heart a second time: *l'éclair*
éclairer, flash of lightning, pastry so light
it's *pâtisserie*. No wonder St. Teresa's
in ecstasy—is it architecture, sculpture
in the round, relief? *In my Father's house*
are many mansions, the many-chambered rose
religieuse at Ladurée, which only proves
Pascal was right—that faith in God is reasonable
because revelation can be comprehended
only by faith, which is justified
by revelation. The icing of the *religieuse*
flows like the folds of a nun's
habit, her robes let loose
like the word for
peony, many-chambered world
without end, each *appoggiatura*
the opposite of apology—not amenable,
without amends, no amen.

Annie Finch

Biographical Sketch

Annie Finch was born in the New York area, and raised in New York and in an isolated camp in the Maine woods. She lives in Falmouth, Maine with her husband, the environmentalist Glen Brand, and their two children. Annie Finch's books of poetry include *Calendars* (2003); *Eve* (1997); and *The Encyclopedia of Scotland* (2004), as well as a translation of the *Complete Poems* of Louise Labé. She has also published a number of books on poetics, including her recent *The Body of Poetry: Essays on Women, Form, and the Poetic Self*. She is Professor of English and Director of the Stonecoast Brief-Residency MFA in Creative Writing at the University of Southern Maine.

Poetry and Earth Spirituality

Poetry was my first spiritual training. For almost as long as I can remember, poetry has guided me to cultivate a life and character open to inspiration, and to discipline myself to the craft of forming poems. As a poet and a pagan, I serve twin Muses—or maybe they are the same: the Muse and the Goddess. It is no surprise that Craft is an ancient term for the religion of the Goddess. As I invent a stanza, match a rhyme, ease a meter through, I feel spiritually connected. Crafting a poem, like weaving a carpet or a shaping a pot, can express the central joys of worship through the creation of a spirited, worthy object.

I have always felt myself to be largely a religious poet, but until I became aware of paganism in recent years I didn't know what kind of religious poet I was. My spiritual yearnings, like those of many pagans or Wiccans, emerged through an ambivalence towards Christianity. Sections of my first book of poetry, *The Encyclopedia of Scotland*—along with poems in *Eve* such as "Running in Church," "Westminster," and "The Door"—

engage with Christian imagery and themes to an extent that surprises to me now, though in retrospect these poems raise pagan-related themes such as the body, nature, female spirituality, and the sacredness of sexuality. "Eve," one of a series of my poems dedicated to goddesses, explores Eve as a transitional figure, both the Eve of Christianity and the mother-goddess figure described in Merlin Stone's *When God Was a Woman*. The imagery of spiral and serpent connects Eve with that older religion and my own spirituality as a woman.

After I became a practicing pagan/Wiccan, I began to write poems to be sung or chanted as part of ceremonies to celebrate the equinoxes, solstices, and other days in the pagan Wheel of the Year. At first, I omitted the ritual songs and the goddess poems from my manuscripts, or segregated them into separate sections. But in the process of putting together first *Eve* and then *Calendars*, I came to see these more chant like poems as integral, even central, to my work.

The sequence of nine goddess poems in *Eve* is a web that links together poems culled from twenty years—and makes it clear how deeply the earlier poems engage with goddess archetypes. In *Calendars*, a sequence of eight poems for the Wheel of the Year, including "Summer Solstice Chant" and "Winter Solstice Chant," delineates and interweaves the thematic resonances of poems from different decades. These chants were originally part of longer pieces that were sung by multiple voices. The long version of "Winter Solstice Chant" was set to music and included imagery of the oak and the ivy, pagan symbols of the birth of the God from the Goddess at this time of year. "Summer Solstice Chant" is part of a chant recited before a ceremony in which written statements of fear and desire are burned in a ritual fire.

I now understand how the pagan focus of the other poems in *Calendars* helps to integrate poetic formalism with experimentalism, and feminism with a sense of humanity. The two interwoven voices in "Earth Goddess and Sky God" express the complementary energies of earth and sky and the perennial mystery that arises between them. Here and in the other multi-voiced poems in the book, the dynamic interplay of forces is probably influenced by the Four Directions and other multivalent pagan concepts. The two other poems included here express a less explicit but equally pagan perspective; "Elegy for My Father" is a deliberately non-Christian elegy invoking the spirit of nature, and "Watching the Whale" a tribute to the spiritual power of nature or the Goddess as manifest in the life of the oceans.

I feel that the timelessness of the pagan themes throughout my work unifies poems from different times in my own life as part of an eternal spiritual present. And my spiritual identity has come to play a central part in my own vision of my poetic mission and vocation. While religions such as Christianity, Judaism, and even Buddhism have many serious poets singing their prayers, I am the only "literary" poet I know of who consciously follows the neopagan path. It is exciting to be helping to shape the literature of a young religion, one so rich in imagery and inspiration, and one I so passionately feel will play a key role in the healing of human lives and of the earth.

EVE

When mother Eve took the first apple down
from the tree that grew where nature's heart had been
and came tumbling, circling, rosy, into sin,
which goddesses were lost, and which were found?
What spirals moved in pity and unwound
across our mother's body with the spin
of planets lost for us and all her kin?
What serpents curved their mouths into a frown,
but left their bodies twined in us like threads
that lead us back to her? Her presence warms,
and if I follow closely through the maze,
it is to where her remembered reaching spreads
in branching gifts, it is to her reaching arms
that I reach, as if for something near to praise.

Watching the Whale

A hard gray wave, her fin, walks out on the water
that thickens to open and then parts open, around her.

Measured by her delved water, I follow her fill
into and out of green light in the depth she has spun

through the twenty-six fathoms of her silent orison,
then sink with her till she rises, lulled with the krill.

Beads of salt spray stop me, like metal crying.
Her cupped face breathes its spouts, like a jewel-wet prong.

In a cormorant's barnacle path, I trail her, spun
down through my life in the making of her difference,

fixing my mouth, with the offerings of silence,
on her dark whale-road where all green partings run,

where ocean's hidden bodies twist fathoms around her,
        making her green-fed hunger grow fertile as water.

Elegy For My Father

HLF, August 8, 1918—August 22, 1997

"Bequeath us to no earthly shore until
Is answered in the vortex of our grave
The seal's wide spindrift gaze towards paradise."
—Hart Crane, "Voyages"

"If a lion could talk, we couldn't understand it"
—Ludwig Wittgenstein

Under the ocean that stretches out wordlessly
past the long edge of the last human shore,
there are deep windows the waves haven't opened,

where night is reflected through decades of glass.
There is the nursery, there is the nanny,
there are my father's unreachable eyes
      turned towards the window. Is the child uneasy?
            His is the death that is circling the stars.

In the deep room where candles burn soundlessly
and peace pours at last through the cells of our bodies,
three of us are watching, one of us is staring
with the wide gaze of a wild, wave-fed seal.
Incense and sage speak in smoke loud as waves,
and crickets sing sand towards the edge of the hourglass.
We wait outside time, while night collects courage
around us. The vigil is wordless. And you

watch the longest, move the farthest, besieged by your breath,
pulling into your body. You stare towards your death,
head arched on the pillow, your left fingers curled.
Your mouth sucking gently, unmoved by these hours
and their vigil of salt spray, you show us how far
you are going, and how long the long minutes are,
while spiralling night watches over the room
and takes you, until you watch us in turn.

Lions speak their own language. You are still breathing.
Here is release. Here is your pillow,
cool like a handkerchief pressed in a pocket.
Here is your white tousled long growing hair.
Here is a kiss on your temple to hold you
safe through your solitude's long steady war;
here, you can go. We will stay with you,
keeping the silence we all came here for.

Night, take his left hand, turning the pages.
Spin with the windows and doors that he mended.
Spin with his answers, patient, impatient.
Spin with his dry independence, his arms
warmed by the needs of his family, his hands
flying under the wide, carved gold ring, and the pages
flying so his thought could fly. His breath slows,
lending its edges out to the night.

Here is his open mouth. Silence is here
like one more new question that he will not answer.
A leaf is his temple. The dark is the prayer.
He has given his body; his hand lies above
the sheets in a symbol of wholeness, a curve
of thumb and forefinger, ringed with wide gold,
and the instant that empties his breath is a flame
faced with a sudden cathedral's new stone.

Winter Solstice Chant

Vines, leaves, roots of darkness, growing,
now you are uncurled and cover our eyes
with the edge of winter sky
leaning over us in icy stars.
Vines, leaves, roots of darkness, growing,
come with your seasons, your fullness, your end.

Summer Solstice Chant

The sun, rich and open,
stretches and pours on the bloom of our work.

In the center of the new flowers,
a darker wing of flower

points you like a fire.

Point your fire like a flower.

Earth Goddess and Sky God

You haven't formed me. I'm a monster still.
Then give me your body. Give it to me in rain.
Look up and fill me. I am too dark to stain.
You haven't held me. I hold apart my will
Spread dryness through me. I have a night to fill
in high heat-speckled waves, apart from where
I will come down. I have nothing to share
with breath. I will give it back. There is one to kill,
one to renew, and one to persuade to weep.
My night holds everything except for sleep.

Patricia Goedicke

Biographical Sketch

Patricia Goedicke: I was brought up in New England by my mother, Helen Mulvey, a graduate of Boston Conservatory of Music, and my father, John B. McKenna, M.D., a jazz piano player, neurologist and psychiatrist at Dartmouth College. After I graduated from Middlebury College (BA) and Ohio University (MA), I and my husband, Leonard Wallace Robinson, a *New Yorker* writer, novelist, and poet, lived and wrote in Mexico for 12 years. In 198I we came to Montana, where I joined the Creative Writing faculty in Missoula and have been teaching and writing (almost 12 books, by now) here ever since, currently as Distinguished Scholar and Professor Emerita of the University of Montana.

Patricia Goedicke's most recent book of poetry, *As Earth Begins to End* (Copper Canyon Press) was recognized by the ALA as one of the year's top ten books of poetry. She taught at the University of Montana, and recent work may be found in *Agni, Colorado Review, Hotel Amerika, Gettysburg Review, Prairie Schooner, Contemporary Northwest Poets Neo,* and *Volt.*

Silence at the Center of Spirituality

I have to say I'm a bit leery of the word "spirituality." There's too much fake that gets attached to it. I believe there's certainly such a thing as "spirit," but all I really know about it is that it's so crucial a thing (if it *is* a "thing") that most people agree it's always what's last to leave the body when it dies. But where does "spirit" go then? Doesn't it, mightn't it simply return, like our fellow animals and plants, to take its place among all the other constantly transformative energies of the universe? I believe that "brightness" does indeed, as Thomas Nashe tells us, "fall from the air"—but what is "brightness"? I believe that whatever is good in our lives is also and at the same time dying; yet I'm still trying to accept all the ramifications of the fact that, in scientific terms, where there's a positive charge there's always a negative charge. *And* vice versa. So, trying to understand how to live in a world full of so much pain and suffering, besides the deep comfort to be found in community, in helping and being helped by others, I look to physics, to biology, to the little I know of Buddhism, and to the far ranging implications of Mandelbrot's dazzling "set." Knowing that I *can't* know what is unknown, I choose to believe that there is as much chance for good in the universe as there is for evil. I look to the various musics of poetry as it has its way with words, those magic carriers of the deep "shocks of recognition" which occur whenever we encounter, in its most penetrating and therefore global form, that elemental embrace of seeming contradictions which constitutes metaphor, poetry's all-important lodestone. Meanwhile, believing that each separate blade of grass, each hair on our heads hums with the same energy as the stars, I look for the silence at the center of things. I watch and I wait. I listen. And sometimes when I am quiet enough, I write.

And Yet

there are so many islands,   sep-
arated
in the brain.
Walk across the channels.   Follow
a sandpiper

Will you be there?

Clearer and clearer, at the edge
where land and sea meet
everywhere, windblown
pebbles
in all corners
and

I see you in the water
the veiled skin of it
cloudy blooms of light
you who disappeared
so many years ago   scattered
dispersed   vaporized
Still here!

Unicycles of the Dead

Overnight the too-late ambulances;
a few more black umbrellas pop up and disintegrate
in small gases, short puffs

now like a rash, now like a bomb cluster of blisters
over the railroad tracks,

see how the fragments come down
delicately?
                    Horrifying as ash. First a femur,
                    then a smile, then an eyelash—

Or crickets, hopscotching.
In and out of the mild
          milky squares we jump around after them,

large suns squeezed into smaller bodies, barely discernable
                    selves like scarred moonscapes seen from within
          and darkening, into thinner and thinner slices

or never. Or right here. Think
kaleidoscopes revolving,
                    opposing parallels that won't stop,

not even for the kindest of saints' countenances dipping
and bowing, pinned to the tall banners

in their royal papier mache processions hiding from us,
                    dodging behind rooftops and cornices vanishing—

*

When it knocks it knocks rapidly. Sharp
one after another stilettos. Machine guns in the distance
                    but coming closer, exploding around us like pillows,
          entire cities of feeling peppered across white sheets —

Yet in a year or two smudged,
out on the lawn grubbing, amiable moles
                    nudging up under us

like footsteps in the backyard,
          strange stepping stones meandering

among white mushrooms sprouting,
faint spores trailing out of sight
                    to the far ends of the galaxies and down Main Street

on All Souls' Night even among witches, even the Mayor as Merlin
with wings flapping, leather overcoats,
sinewy swallow tails silhouetted

as benign blips, UFO's whiz by
off the memory screen into stale candy
in numb brain pockets rubbing dully against us—

*

And then easier:
Though the smell is of slick, broken
thick finger bones, the whiplash of loose lightning
jabbing at the horizon,

they keep coming, but softer.
In the taste of twilight cigarettes drifting
across the grass like Myrmidons, hobos at the back door

whether we notice them or not, they keep tapping,
behind the eyes whispering, each night and not just in the movies,
a series of serious men and grave women in top hats
on skinny unicycles wobbles across the sky and disappears

over and over, but the world's windows are transparent,
the couple across the way forever yaps at each other
over their tea-time martinis, with the cat snoring in the corner
later they make love, shedding inhibitions and clothing

everywhere, as small flecks of bare skin scoot
under the sofa and the refrigerator, even after they move on they remain

in pieces all over the house, in bureau drawers,
in desks. On the back stairs, especially in the glassy negative,
the whirlpool depths of mirrors
continually changing places, out there

all around us on the dark lawns rustling, shifting back and forth
where the leaving, the left behind, the finally lost still live.

Aftermath: Pinpoint and Torrent

A black dot, far away. The prick
and needled hiss of it. And the trickling, here on the beach
as sky narrows to pupil. Garish

at the end of every light-shift
what's left but empty?

Gulled from the shore. As grackles shoot from a tree
shredded skirts rise. Black ash

flaps from a burning funeral pier;
smell of incensed seaweed.

As grit flies across wave crash, far from abraded flesh
perspective's point dwindles to a flat horizon.

picketed by grief's scabs
all gathers to a cry: rasp of seashells scraping.
Slow. Implacable. Grinding, O

buffaloed, hurled from a mesa.
Slaughtered spirits extinct to what we don't know,

in the plod of daily bread we beg for it:
resurrection, *consummation*
of the cindered body passionately to be

aroused. Born again into skin, into its own
multiply seething corpuscles somehow
returned, returned—but No,

obviously. Cold slap in the face. Because living
or dead no one's home
anyway, just left

seconds ago, out the door to the beach,
among the dunes glittering
beyond all scatter as vast
diamond pitted flakes scratch against each other–

(loud silence
of ants sipping water,
brittle grasshoppers breathing)—

As in a tape recorder's low
whispered undertow a flicked snare drum's ghost

taps in and out, the foaming
scrolled wheelbarrow of a once
deep baritone voice attenuates itself

beyond the beach,
from a stuttering cassette bodiless, its frayed edges
keep flickering; on, off

to the outer eye motionless, in each cell
the mind's remembering dendrites fly by
faster than any instrument can measure—

As riddled pinpoints flash, reactivated
static reflects what was
and still is, in bright cascading sparks

tiny geysers jet across small
empty intersections; plus, minus, positive
and negative, both as each speck splashes

for a few milliseconds in a circle scratched by a star
on a blind eye, the tail end of a smile

across the water gathers to zero and then fizzes
into the abyss of it, radiant
black pinhole, torrent and vortex twisting

yes, where we converge
in the aftermath, with everything slowly settling

and then rising, no surcease—

yet in the black sea of it, its syllables (strings in the wind)
in the frantic spittle of matter
                                        in constant motion streaming,

in the watery spaces between us, cool sibillants
spit air and speak up:

stumbling along Oceanside Boulevard, listen,
even in strobed tears, between jeweled lightning shafts, *don't cry,*

as oblivion's traffic whines, hisses, sucks
all of us—quarks, taus, muons, *human beings—*
                                                            into its bright grit churning

like mangled shorebirds, in the crash, whiplash and
jerk of convertibles, shiny steel caskets
        with their heads lopped off, *don't stop, look up*

go for the bull's eye, sight
right through it, pin the transparent

                                                    black and white negative to the bull's eye.

Dennis Hinrichsen

Biographical Sketch

Dennis Hinrichsen: I was born in Cedar Rapids, Iowa, downwind of a Quaker Oats plant that overwhelmed our city summer days with the sweet smell of sorghum. The oldest of four children—two sisters and one brother—I had a kind of Huck Finn childhood complete with jackknife, fishing pole, 20-inch Schwinn bike, and free run of the city. Somehow, I survived. This continued through two stints in Illinois, a return to Iowa, before settling in Michigan, where I live now (after a decade in the Boston area) with my wife and lone cat.

Dennis Hinrichsen's most recent work is *Cage of Water* (University of Akron Press 2004), and *Message to Be Spoken into the Left Ear of God* (Mayapple Press 2004). He lives and teaches in Lansing, Michigan where he also is coeditor of *Review Revue*, a journal of prosody essays, book reviews, and interviews with poets.

Spirituality and Poetry

A passage from John Cage's "Lecture on Nothing" from *Silence* comes to mind when I think about spirituality and poetry:

> It is not irritating to be where one is . It is only irritating to think one would like to be somewhere else.

The key word, of course, is "irritating," a condition (or pre-condition) the essay delightfully tests again and again and perhaps even builds in the reader through the middle section of the lecture/poem.

As I often misremember the piece, other words silt in like *dissatisfaction*, *unease*, that speak to our drive for transcendence for in the end, the poem concludes, the moment spills. How could it be otherwise? And so we haul ourselves from sacred space to sacred space, building from the materials at hand whatever we can with imagination and vision. Knowing full well that whatever we fashion is provisional. This seems to me to be our practice, and our pleasure, as Cage would say. Again from "Lecture on Nothing":

Everybody has a song
which is no song at all:
it is a process of singing
and when you sing ,
you are where you are

Viewing the Holy Ghost, Horseshoe Canyon

And then, suddenly, this body: all ochre,
ground hematite,
adrift on a rock

expanse: a spiritual,
precise graffiti,
the face of god thrown,

finally, in the name of mud
(the binding agent:
organic, unknown);

some of it painted, pecked;
some of it
dribbled and left to run

(snake in real time,
a desert bull,
sliding its black-braided water

through dust and grass,
my body laid,
sacrificial, on a heated stone).

I could hear it stop—the snake—
sift again
the coarseness—

aridness etched; each serrated blade
of time—
some of me blown

like mist from the mouth…
exploding star,
all paint and spittle. Dimensionality

(sweat streaking an upper check)
like a sect mark,

the way the Holy Ghost is marked,

was marked (our name/
their image)
2000 b.c.e. And so he strides,

Barrier Canyon Style,
out of sheered flatness
into a pool of shade—

an armless, legless spirit prowling
the threshold.
Iterations of the kinetic;

sacred. So that hiking out
of the canyon
even the ravens were part of it—

one crying black streaks
into that penetrable,
massive silence;

stalling in effortless down-swoop
before a gap
in the rock;

then swift, cursive upleap—
wings
spread—wings dampened…

balance at the nest's lip.
The other raven
shrieking. Taking mouth

from mouth—raven kiss,
raven breath,
twig bit; a weight-

lessness: desert silk. Because
who
wouldn't want, in the end,

the unlikeness to roll away, and
                the artistry
        arise : goat, god, sheep; human, human.

Crazy Horse Mountain

Uprootedness is what I wanted—out of the ground
                of my skin
        a fierce yanking—

so that later I was disappointed at first,
                and then
        reluctantly blessed, when the Sioux warrior,

counting coup, tapped my arm
                for Jesus. Christ,
        how I'd spent years dodging

that chrome icon, my sins in his fist,
                my body
        elsewhere: a vine twisting along a rusty nail.

And so I thought: whose God then?
                Whose spirit
        driven like a pony before the wind?

It was all play, of course—*I am*
                quicker than you, braver—
        but still, I wanted

to leap up and strike him back, wave
                the ceremonial wing—
        a violation?—

like healing smoke

        *

toward holiness…

And so I ate the fry bread, tuned in
to Hank Williams
all morning,

stood before the quartz stalks
of Crazy Horse's eyes
(who was never photographed)

and let myself be stolen—
Nikon, Pentax;
digital, video—

my flesh spirit mixed with stone spirit
dynamited
from rock

taken in strands like spider's silk,
or braided rope—
a crash

*

and reckless fountaining…

O Shirtwearer, Curly, Light Hair,
His Horse Stands in Sight,

where is that warrior now,
the one you dreamed,
who took no scalps,

spoke little, dressed plainly,
zigzag lightning
marking his cheek,

hail dotting the body, rider shaken so fiercely
his loose hair
was the wing of a hawk…

Just now, the moon

*

has let fly its glass horse
over the Dakotas,

filling the campsite with arctic light,
though the air
is 90, and the tent

is folding like my mind
with the wind.
Sometimes lying down so flat

it shimmers—like a mirage, or water.
Sometimes swelling like a lung.
I'll have to weigh

its weathered fabric with two or three
heavy stones—
to anchor sleep—

or wait until the stars come out,
trickster-flung,
and let their milky wash recast me.

Coyote Bliss

High summer, interstate: in the mile after I'd dropped
you off, there
was a body, one of god's dogs,

at the road's side, contradictory and ambiguous,
its gross physical
sheathing about to burst through

its sheath of intelligence,
whatever was left
of it, its sheath of bliss.

Still the animal held its carriage,
skin and body,
bone, so much a part of the landscape

I cannot think without it: paws
held rigid
as if to repel the sun: song fragments,

fragments of its trace,
from restlessness to abiding,
its last pained yip, hurt howl.

Elsewhere, once,
I bent
to touch another's left forepaw ridged

in mud, New Mexico desert, off-trail
creek-bed,
mustard yellow stone chalked

so perfectly into the surrounding hillsides
it was a remnant
of wind, wind's upswept tail.

Some sovereign mineral whispering
to the form
I was, and nudging. And so I let it nudge.

I dreamed blue fire, ghost of water,
paw print,
coyote saving the bones for O'Keeffe
(O'Keeffe painting the bones), the fragments
resting upon,
the clouds between fragments

until the wind picked up
                    and was stone
          again, and I shook myself dusty

in its thrashing. Looked for snakes. Thought
                    again of that other
          rabid creature I walked twice past

on the Canyon's south rim as if
                    to ruin
          my life, to fuck it up, fuck it royally,

chaos soaking me in saffron, coyote
                    (seen by the eyes
          of God) working the scrub…

On the flight back: storm front, a hundred or so
                    miles of it,
          lightning breaking like glass at 20,000 degrees

in a living animal's eye, forest line
                    down below
          exploding with dusk, whole acres ripped

to fiery plumes, though I could not
                    hear them
          above the engine's constant mechanical

whirr—inside my head like a wind,
                    like a trail,
          like a scent… I thought: I, too, shall fly

home. I shall eat well (eat anything), sing planet on fire.

Richard Jackson

Biographical Sketch

Richard Jackson was born in Lawrence, MA, taught high school in North Adams, MA, and then went on to graduate school at Yale for his PhD. He travels to Europe a couple of times a year taking writing students from UT-Chattanooga where he teaches. His biblical monologues are an effort to understand some of the more difficult issues of our time.

Richard Jackson is the author of nine books of poems, most recently *Half Lives* (Autumn House) *Unauthorized Autobiography* (Ashland Poetry Press) and *Heartwall* (University of Mass). He is the winner of Guggenheim, Fulbright, and Witter Bynner fellowships, 5 Pushcart Appearances, and awards from *Prairie Schooner, Crazyhorse* and other journals. He is also the author of two books of criticism and several chapbooks. His poems have been translated into a dozen languages, and he teaches at UT-Chattanooga and Vermont College's MFA program.

Role of Spirituality

In some ways the poet takes a cue from Ezekiel 37, where the prophet is transported (much like the poet's inspiration) to the valley of dry bones and commanded to make them live again by speaking. As a result they assemble themselves—in an act that is echoed when the poet pulls his materials together. The prophet then commanded to speak to the wind, and, as a result, the breath, the soul, enters the bodies that have risen. I think that this scene reflects what the poet or anyone who wants to understand the creative process senses: disparate elements are joined together, as Samuel Johnson said of the metaphysical poets. All my poems start in a sensual world on a sensual level—the level of bones and flesh—but they quickly move on to questions about love, forgiveness, hope, death and such things, often from the point of view of a biblical character. In the poems in this anthology, my speakers try to defend themselves and offer a critique of our own world that has been mired in a gross materialism and lack of values.

The Lesson of Samson

What do you do when your shadow is more exact than
Your own self? When your own secrets sleep in your throat?
Even the nightingale sings what it collects from the day's
failures. There was a time when everything pleased me,
When everything called my name. That was before I lived
In a landscape someone else invented. Later, I never found
Any certain record of what I was supposed to do,
Or why. I was an echo with no first sound. I was alone.
Yes, it's true, Deliah was only the last of too many
Lovers. Inside them, the folds of the universe seemed to
Cover me like silk. I went to them because
My own wife betrayed my secret to her friends.
That's why I dragged the burning fox through their fields.
In the end, we weave our own pain into our lives.
That's why I believe my own shadow felt the wound
when they burned her alive as a kind of revenge,
an act you think savage, but look at your own dirty wars.
We live by symbols and gestures whose meaning
Drifts like leaves on the wind. So maybe the lion meant me,
the honey what she could have been. Whatever my life was
supposed to mean crested too far out to sea. Whoever wrote
my story said my own revenge was the hand of God.
Then why the symbol of the jawbone? He said I brought
down the temple of the Infidels, but who is to say
that their souls did not bud like flowers in the fields?
In truth, no revenge, no cause is that noble.
In truth, anyone's knees will bend like stalks of wheat.
Now your own soldiers warm their hands over the bodies
Of children in Angola or my own Palestine.
The hoot of the owl tells us all what we have lost.
And me, I have only these lidless eyelids of desire
To guide me. All I can do now is mimic the roots
That finger, like lovers, the desert sands for water.
Antlers of smoke rise from the cities I razed.
Fear darts in and out of the cellars and ditches.
What did it mean? What could any of us expect?
In the end, they all go back to their idols, their rapes,

Their revenge, their bayonets waving like flags.
My own face is covered by the sheet of the sky.
Reason leaks from my wounds. A life is not a life until you die.

Ruth's Advice

Did it matter if my blood was streaked like one of
those streams that stumble by your rusted factories?
Did it matter that the sun passed above me on a stretcher?
I stepped into the field like a field until he nearly
tripped over me. You know nothing of real solitude —
your stories and your mirrors keep you company.
Why can't you go wherever your love goes, live
wherever your love lives? There's too much you want
to strap to yourself like a suicide bomber's pack.
You can't invest your soul. You can't invest your love.
It wasn't my grain but what that grain could mean.
In the end all our lives are strewn across the road
like curls of some truck's blown tire. What's to salvage?
Sometimes you don't even know what you thirst for.
You think you could drink from the puddle of the moon.
You think you can give yourself over to the wind.
Don't you think the bed sheets scorched my skin?
I lay at his feet and, startled, he covered me. I put
my mouth to his heart. The night tilted away from us.
We used to hurl our words against the door to keep out robbers.
I became one of you. You became one of me. But
I never understood how you could hang someone's words
like bloated fruit from a tree. How you could refuse someone
a place to sit. Don't let the ink of those laws still stain
your soul. The polls of the heart are still open. Each time
you refuse, the past scratches its name into your walls.
Your old habits grab their canes for support. Let them go.
When you don't, even your signature deserts you.
I remember a time when the birds seemed to have
no place to land. I remember a time when I thought
I'd have to peddle my life on some street corner.
Though it was long ago, I can tell you he loved me,
his people loved me despite the place I came from,

despite my name. At first I feared the future as if it were
one of your eighteen wheelers jackknifing in front of me.
What could love do? I worried. Now my hopes thrum like
the cable of this elevator. It's a long ways up.
The ambulances of desire are racing down your streets.
Yes, these comparisons are over the top, I know, but there
you are, still there nursing your old intentions like a drink.
It's after midnight. Open the door. Whatever's there
will grab you by the shoulder and turn you around.

Cain's Legacy

You can't stop the boxcars of despair.
You can't stop my voice from hiding out
like a virus inside your words, their knives
clamped between your teeth. You can't stop
the dogs gnawing on the bones from mass graves.
Thus your mirrors holding other faces. Thus your lungs
filled with someone else's words.
The eyelids of the heart closing. The sky drunk
on vapor trails. Otherwise, a few packages of conscience
to the refugees. You can't stop the sounds
of exploding stars as they approach you.
The anxious triggers. The land mines of idealism.
You can't stop Dismay from stumbling
out of the trenches of your dreams.
You can't stop these ghosts sitting around your table
gnawing on the past. Their candles burn down
to shimmering wounds in their cups.
Everyone holding their favorite flags like napkins.
The sound of bugles spilling from the room like laughter.
I know, you kill what you love just to hate yourself
all the more. You put on the cloak of distance.
A wind that blows away the weeks. The lovers' wilted embrace
that was your only, your last hope.
Everyone his own Judas. After a while
even the moon is just an excuse not to look too closely.
You can't stop the past boiling up in the heart like lava.
Otherwise, a history written by shadows.

For example, someone says the universe is expanding,
more anxious optimism, but where would it expand into?
There's only the vacuum that's always inside us.
There's Stephen Hawking saying the past is pear shaped
but that doesn't feed anyone. You can't stop the brain
of the starving child turning into a peach pit,
not his body terrorizing itself for food,
not his face wrinkling like the orange you leave on your table,
his liver collapsing, the last few muscles snug
over his bones like the tight leather gloves of your debutante.
Otherwise your old lies yawning to wake in the corner.
You can't stop the pieces of the suicide bomber
from splattering all over the cafe walls.
You can't stop the walls the tanks crush from rising again.
Otherwise a few tired rivers, a few fugitive stars.
The seasons that ignore us. The cicadas giving up on us.
Hope's broken antennas. Love trying to slip out of the noose.
The betrayed lives we were meant to live.
You can't stop that town from turning its soul on a spit,
not the light chiseling away desire, the morning
wandering dazed through the underbrush of deception.
You can't stop these sails of tomorrow hanging limp
from their masts. All you have are these backwaters of touch,
this voice spinning like a broken compass,
this muzzle made from your own laws.
But you can't stop the bodies piling up.
You can't stop the deafening roar of the sky.
You can't stop the bullet you've aimed at your own head.

Tidings

1. The Annunciation

Like a sentence you discover and read after too many
years, after you think the world's heart has turned
to dust, the air shriveling in your lungs, though
you cannot understand some of the words
for they seem like stars with no owners,
something like the ache of flowers for their seeds,

and you begin to realize it is a sentence
that celebrates what you could only imagine
like the canticles of mountain streams,
despite the black hearts perched, years later, on branches,
despite the moon thinning with hunger
then bloating like a starving child,
despite the tracer rounds streaming
like dandelion seeds the Child will blow across His room,
this sentence with its riverbed of stars,
this sentence that carries you too
the way a leaf is pulled downstream, because this,
you begin to realize, is not the song of a seed
fallen on stone, not some light scorched
into the dunes of the sky, but a phrase
whose wings fill the room, and you, —
you are that word which had remained
unnoticed in this sentence, and you begin
to speak with that light that quivers
like a branch, your own lips slightly moving
like a petal the bee has just left,
and you begin to realize you have lived
your whole life in this sentence
gradually unfolding towards its end,
the way the moon now plows the sky,
the way what you once thought was a mere star
now turns out to be a galaxy.

2. Three Kings

The sound was all yellow, the flower of the moon
opened. For a while we thought we were living
in the landscape of someone else's dream.
There was a fire that burned like an icicle from a rope.
Someone else said it might be a star.
He seemed to know something about the moon's scars,
so we followed. We tracked the ruts of the sky's song.
You can cut off the branches of a dogwood and still
see its outlines in the air. Sometimes our gaze
just crawled along the road carrying a burden
we somehow wanted. We knew how tight
the chains of our hearts held us.

When we went to the king you could hear the stars wilt.
We thought he wanted to tear the clouds from the sky.
The winds gathered in the mountains, plotting.
We could hear the cry of the trees, the desperate
snail clinging to a rock. Later we heard
the the voice of mothers raging over the hills
like the glow of a fire. Everyone we met wanted
to blindfold the sky. It seemed their were clocks
inside their hearts. It seemed their eyes
were made of dust. When we finally arrived
it was as if we could see every blade of grass,
every seed's beginning, every cricket's song,
every star's desire. And then we could speak.
It seemed His words opened our own mouths.
Here was the universe in a husk of song.
Here was a city in a splinter of joy.
Here were our souls embracing like our smoky breaths.
Here was pure hope flowering in His eyes.

3. Joseph

And so the stars finally pelted us
with answers. Whatever tears we had were pressed
like olives. He came quietly then,
a stirring in the frost, a shuffling of the lamb's feet.
When the cold settled on his eyelids
it was if a flock of doves lowered their quilt
down around us. It was then we knew that
the stars only wanted to drink from the pools
they seemed to live in, or become the insects
you could hear above the heartbeats of animals.
It was like lifting a stone to see another world,
a stone we had carried all that time.
Now the whole story will appear like the exposed roots
of a dogwood. Hope collects like dew in the desert night.
Even the hanged man will strangle his ropes.
It is our swords that will plow the sky.
Our lives are thumb prints in the air, which means
that soon all our dreams will wander on without us.

Our graves will fill their sails with light.
You can open their words like almonds.
You have to step into that river that flows inside you.
It is a world where suns are sown like seeds.
It is not easy, this beating your wings against the world.
Even now you can see the fingertips of His words
starting to knead the air into the shape of a prayer,
a sentence inscribed in your eyes that only you can read.

Mia Leonin

Biographical Sketch

Mia Leonin: I am half Cuban and half American. Born and raised in Missouri, matured in Miami (thirteen years now). I'm a Gemini. I live with my partner Carlos, daughter Rafaela and my mother, Norma.

Mia Leonin's book of poems *Braid* was published by Anhinga Press. Her second collection *The Repeating Garden* is forthcoming from Anhinga. She has been awarded an Academy of American Poets Prize. In 2005, she was the recipient of a Florida Individual Artist Fellowship.

Conversion to Poetry

Sundays, my mother liked to "rest her eyes," but she insisted I go to church and in our small Missouri town, the options were legion. By the time I was twelve, my skinny legs had swung from the pews of the Christian, Baptist, and Methodist churches to name a few. Some Sundays, two busses would pull up to our drive way and start honking. I would peek out the window anxiously. "Just get on one," my mother sighed, "There all heading to the same place." After attending some thirteen churches, I had to agree. I alternated between bouts of anxiety that my growling stomach might be heard over the preacher to long stretches of boredom, where my fidgeting fingers would inevitably discover an old wad of chewing gum—or worse. Finally, my mother conceded to letting me stay home and read the Bible, thus beginning my conversion to poetry.

Magdalena

My Room

He touched my hair to the curtain.
I asked the child to choose a candle.
I asked the man to choose his position.

They both chose San Martín and me on my knees
My back turned to every corner of the room.

Flute: shade growing up the mountain.
Morning stitched into the window.

The man wrapped his hand around the boy's wrist
And guided him up the river, the candle sputtering,
The flame approaching.

Waiting out these yellow days I think of them
The man and his son—taking a tour of the Nile
Envious of the moon—the both of them

Jealous of my morning tree edged with late afternoon light,
Even jealous of my silver bracelets,
How they were pounded from solitude.

The Promise

My mother told me not to look for him—

The golden one carrying his face in a bottle
The one whose pink fingers open and close like a newborn's mouth
The one trembling beneath his freshly sharpened knife.

She told me not to look for him—

The one who floats within his own pockets.
The one with crushed eucalyptus leaves in his hair
The one whose promises bleed into his sandals.

My Face

Wherever he is, I will outlive his oldest robe.
I am at that age—ripe for a young man—a delight for the old one.
I am always that age

My Mat

Midnight, a suture in my robe.
Only room for one on this mat.

Where else is there to wait
But beneath clavicle and thumbs?

I turn myself back like a starched sheet.
I pull them in, slide them under, wrap them inside.
I lay them on my stomach like a rug.

This mat that has carried so many
Has only room for one. Call me Mother,
Call me Magdalene, Apostle, Eve.

Mother Tongue

I wear white, so you will open me
And find the letter, addressed

To your next country of origin,
Spoken in your new native language.

Your tongue is both lava and led—molten and mercurial.
From Spanish to English you go. From German to French,

Each word a greedy cockroach hoarding its own meaning,
Each metaphor a bee mistaking itself for a deity.

Words are not born. We are born into speaking.
I too lean in to celebrate my own precious phonics.

I speak of my mother's memoried village: a white sheet hung
On her wedding night to broadcast love's first bloody syllable.

The village retreats into its architecture, a man
Stands in a field, searching for his shadow among corn.

This is the home our tongues point to when we are talking,
The nest, when we are quiet and without feathers.

At best, we are onomatopoeia, brightly colored words
Limping after the original, the inanimate.

Memory of Fire

Longing
Not to be a god or a hero, but a tree
To grow for ages, not hurt anyone.

Czeslaw Milosz

When I was a child, something burned
Something smelled of flowers
Something glowed of organdy and hickory.

Ojalá

Breezes, dresses burning
Orange, organdy flames
Licking up my mother's legs.

On the days she prayed, I watched her hair
Spill around her face.
God tumbled into pieces at her knees
And she gathered him in her dress.

On the days she didn't pray, I approached her with little notes
Where I tried to make the "o" in Mommy wink
Or the "y" curl like the stem of a flower.

What are you doing, Mommy? I read the note to her.
Resting my eyes. And it was true.
She never opened them.

I waited for the game show bells at 6:30.
I turned up the volume as high as it would go.
She would jump up and paint on Cleopatra eyes.

Sometimes she lit votive cups and sent me outside.
Sometimes she raced me to Dairy Queen.
Sometimes we poured turquoise rocks into a glass bowl
And dreamed of water.

Ojalá

When I was a child, something burned
Something smelled of flowers
Something glowed of organdy and hickory.

We moved constantly and without conviction
Always within the same three-room house.

I stood in the front yard and watched the screen door
Fly open and spit out our possessions—bottle opener, can opener,
Corkscrew, screwdriver.

Ojalá

The hours crowded around my tent of leaves.
From the willow, I learned to stand still amidst so much weeping.

I leaned for hours—my arms stretching out
My wrists staring past the sky.

Thirteenth Apostle

1.

Bastards.

I was there.

Judas' spirit hovered like the hood of a cobra.
Between the new eye of sun and the cock's crow
Peter coiled four times.

I stood close enough to see people tear at him,
As if his skin were robes. I watched them stick their fingers
Into the mouth of his wound.

2.

In one cry, every parable flew from his throat.
Even as the body stiffened to its cross,
People cried *Magician! Demon!*
Some insisted his teachings weren't possible without him.

Isn't a word when torn from the loaf still bread?
They didn't sacrifice their warmest part
To his feet. They didn't wind the lament
Of his robes around their hands.

For three days, I broke the alabaster vase of balm
Across my forehead—a lightening. No end. No origin.
After such a storm, only willows.

3.

My kisses can sew your palms shut. Blasphemy.
Can it be true even now
I try to break up men's pain
With my body? After everything,
Is the wound my only tool?

Repentance, I open my thoughts,

Peeling the leaves of my intentions,

Throwing away the brown, fondling
The green and cool.

I wait for the sun to set and with it,
Plant my knees in your garden of asphalt,
In your garden of red dirt, sand, and pasture.

I have been every color, every shape.
Each time I return I am dropped into the light,
Naked and bald.
My hair is my only memory.
With each birth, I grow it out again.

4.

Eucharist, I am restored
By the body. Not hands or prayer or scripture.

Jesus, you must be in me
Because I never sleep. You dictate
Emptying the alabaster jars,
Turning them, over and over.

Flock of one lamb,
Congregation of one. I kneel
Outside the church and love
In all the wrong ways.

I bow my head and let my hair fall
Anoint the feet of all the sinners
Who might be saviors.

Timothy Liu

Biographical Sketch

Timothy Liu was born and raised in San Jose, California. He served a Mormon mission in Hong Kong, and then returned to earn a B.A. at Brigham Young University and an M.A. at the University of Houston. Liu lives in New York City.

Timothy Liu is the author of six books of poems, most recently *For Dust Thou Art* (Southern Illinois, 2005) and *Of Thee I Sing* (Georgia, 2004). His poems have been translated into seven languages, and his journals and papers are archived in the Berg Collection at the New York Public Library. An Associate Professor at William Paterson University and a member of the Core Faculty in Bennington College's Graduate Writing Seminars, Liu lives in New York City.

Statement

Death is not only the mother of Beauty but the broker of our future spiritual estate. Our birthright? To be betrayed by our bodies in the end. If there is something beyond our earthly material existence that we presently navigate in the flesh, then isn't it through the use of spiritual tools that we come to inquire after the invisible? Religion. Philosophy. Poetry. Those metaphysical instruments we turn to by which we make contact with whatever cannot be perceived by the five senses alone. And as our bodies decay, surely our spiritual aptitudes evolve? In the beginning was the Word, and the Word was with God, and the Word was God. John's gospel invocation. But in the end? Will even the Word abandon us, or at least the words we employ? Redemption. Atonement. Salvation. The poem as a kind of stand-in for elusive Love even when faced with intolerable Loss.

And Their Sins Shall Be While as Snow

The town's five baseball diamonds neatly groomed.

Verging into solipsistic terror.

Hay-loft hanky panky as the hat goes round.

With boredom at the root.

Tract homes across America approximating field.

Holiday malls strung out in Xmas lights.

Purveyors of a terra incognita.

Human travail.

Trapped in a moral hell but making beauty just as well.

And Not for Any Other Name Would I Have Come

Who are you who tunnel your way
into this knowing whom I do not know unseemly
looking through my own eyes at yourself
looking back and
I
asking for nothing but
my own eyes back yet I see nothing
except these borrowed
distortions of the self seen through another
window raised
against the night the day the night
returning with untimely
delay that ripens
meanings in a body playing host to my exhausted
ass unable to deflect
recurrent thrusts everyone said would cost
too much and yet
I pay for this for only in this
nothingness would the god disclose his ruined face—

Called to Serve Him

at whatever cost even as communion

did them in—kisses all sty and hurry
mired to archaic raunch—godly hum

pillowing boys to sleep where dreams

collapsed—love's awkward stutters
unsure of speech leveled by whispers

hand over mouth as love flooded in—

The Desert Fathers

Singing hymns which had more scope
than a one kiloton nuke. Thirteen million

dead from AIDS—the life expectancy

in Botswana less than forty years of age.
Wiping out an entire nation. Not for lack

of drugs had we come for this: emotion-

laden buggery levied against God's word—
a world at odds with a go-as-you-please

self-serving style, the sacred rendered

void. As meanings can be mean, choose
ye this day windfall hopes proscribed

in medias res—cadential points cobbled

together for emotional effect—jazzed-up
jihad mufti muzaked through the roof.

Extreme Unction

For lovers emptied of their kiss a dream undone.

Reduced to this old bell as sinners kneel.

Hammers breaking stone to birth the arms and lips.

Toiling today for tomorrow's bread.

His body unadorned but garment to the bride.

His bare hands world enough.

Drunk on prayer as he rode me to the nethermost.

Like a Dog to His Own Vomit

Washed in the blood of Christ, you emerge

anew but for the old blood pumping still
to reassert itself long after the novelty has

worn off. His body all verb-studded excess.

The spirit is strong but the flesh is weak!
Or was it the other way around? You can't

remember last week's sermon, only some

hell to pay—aversive therapy strapping
your dick to a chair, electrodes firing up

like bloods from the 'hood scoring joints

from a Mister Softee van, each strung out

and growing fat on violence at the local

mall till someone shoots a look your way

as if meaning to say: "The management
regrets to inform you that your patronage

is no longer appreciated." What selves

we have ceded to make our own occult
composite of regret, our icons traded-in

for ivy leaves ironed-on a frat boy's briefs.

My Last Night on Rhodes

A blood moon waning above the Cretan sea,

the rhododendrons stirring less as the Meltemi
dies down. Yes, there are tourists, but where

are there not tourists, and I among them, happy

to discover that the Greek I daily butcher
is not required in this place where they speak

in my own tongue. An island nowadays seems

little more than the people on it, but hasn't that
always been true? No one around here claims

to own the moon—ah—isn't that the beauty

of a place where you can slowly peel back all
the layers—ruin upon ruin—a crumbling mosque

where a Byzantine church once stood after

pulling down a pagan temple whose columns

are still intact if you dig down deep enough

in a place where little of anything else survives,

I think, on my last night on Rhodes, happy
for the simple fact that I'm able to leave

not a single trace of my lonesome self behind—

Denise Low

Biographical Sketch

Denise (Dotson) Low of Lawrence, Kansas, has lived in the same house almost 30 years, and so has watched transformations of seasons and decades—with a white pine, a ponderosa, a maple still standing. She grew up in the Flint Hills, 85 miles to the southwest and regularly visits them. She feels that all the wisdom of the world can be read in the text of the land and sky. Her children are David Low, a wine maker (Anthill Farms of Sonoma Co.); Daniel Low, an attorney with Boies, Schiller & Flexner in D.C.; and a stepdaughter Pemy Wesosa Fleuker, who works with a NASA grant. Her husband Thomas Pecore Weso, Menominee Nation member, is an adjunct professor at Longview Community College in Lee's Summit, MO. Her sister is the well known writer, Jane Ciabattari.

Denise Low is chair of the English Department at Haskell Indian Nations University, where she also teaches creative writing and American Indian Studies. Her recent book *Words of a Prairie Alchemist,* essays and interview excerpts, is from Ice Cube Press (2006), and she edited *Wakarusa Wetlands in Word & Image* for the Lawrence Arts Center's Imagination & Place Committee (2005). *Thailand Journal: Poems* was named a notable book of 2003 by the *Kansas City Star,* and her *New & Selected Poems 1980-1999* (Penthe Press). She was guest co-editor of *Teaching Leslie Marmon Silko's* Ceremony, a special issue of *American Indian Culture and Research Journal*, UCLA, 28.1 (2004). Her articles, essays, and reviews of American Indian literature appear in *Studies in American Indian Literature, American Indian Culture and Research Journal, American Indian Quarterly, Midwest Quarterly*, and *Kansas City Star*. She is a 5th generation Kansan of mixed German, Scots, Lenape (Delaware), English, French, and Cherokee heritage, and a member of the Prairie Writers Circle of The Land Institute.

Fragmentary Belief Systems

Perhaps because of my mixed heritage, I find my beliefs derived from my immediate environment rather than a fixed ideology. Joseph Campbell speaks of this historic era as one of religious "terminal moraines." By this he means many fragmentary belief systems are mixed together, out of time, on the North American continent. I celebrate the Indigenous American peoples who retain continuous occupation of their lands and also sustain their languages and cultures into this era. As a descendant of scattered peoples, I do not have this fortune.

Since I was young, I have turned to processes of nature for instruction and sustenance. I grew up within the Flint Hills, one of the last stands of the continent's grasslands, and the scale of the sky inspired me beyond the flat ceiling of my parents' Congregational Church. I imagined eternity by watching red tail hawks spiral upwards, and I glimpsed mortality when finding scattered bones in the soil. Weather, seasons, sites, stars, and creatures all provide texts of life patterns. Cityscapes also follow natural laws in their own forms, so streets of towering buildings resemble canyon walls. Human-created forms cannot exist outside of gravity. This is not a pastoral romanticism, but rather a law of physics.

Attempts at reconstructing natural forms in language sustain my quest for balance and serenity. Writing is a spiritual discipline that improves those who learn and follow its laws—which are not separate from nor different from other laws of nature.

Menominee Rez, Sunday Morning

Church bells ring and rez dogs
sing tenor. We cross St. Joseph's
back to the forest, past two boys
rolling toy trucks in a yard.
Peals and wolf howls rise
like drifting pine smoke.

At the logging road we find
a buffalo- nickel key ring
and Marine Corps tags.
Ripe cattails ring a dry pond
where seven clans gathered
years before French Sundays.

Last night, stars streaked
the black void but now blue
spreads thin like a Great Lake
misplaced in the sky. Sun burns
through needles, silent
yet piercing all our eyes.

Rough-Legged Hawk: Iowa

Fare thee well at once;
The Glow-worme showes the Matine to be neere,
And gins to pale his uneffectuall Fire:
Adue, adue, Hamlet: remember me.
- Shakespeare

Spirits of the dead rustle
In my left ear. *Remember me.*
Remember me. In half-light
an owl sifts through time
on glider wings. Sunset.
Ghosts become shadows
stooped behind mounds

of moraine and corn stubble.
My dead niece shakes
her veil of black wavy hair
across my face and I smell
her musk, her lost beauty.
My father-in-law brings
another jade necklace
and forgives me.
Solstice. Sunset.

In dim illumination
another vision sharpens.
My mother rises and walks.
My grandmother, who outlived
everyone she knew, limps,
sapphire eyes still on fire.
Friends appear, and a child.
Then horizons fold over.

Tree limbs reach heaven,
un-leafed. Black hawks sit high
rearranging feather cloaks.
They follow winter
even to this far frostline.
Quick movements snap their eyes.
Sunfall and pale glow-worm dawn
they harvest fruits of the dark.

American Robin

Nothing would give up life:
Even the dirt kept breathing a small breath.
-Theodore Roethke

Cold sun brings this mourning season to an end—
One year since my mother's death. Last winter thaw
my brother shoveled clay-dirt, she called it gumbo,
over what the crematorium sent back. Not her,
but fine powdery substance, lightened, all else

rendered into invisible elements. That handful
of a pouch, un-boxed, was tucked into plotted soil,
the churchyard columbarium, a brass plaque the only

permanence, and the brick retaining wall. So finally
my mother is a garden, day lilies and chrysanthemums
feeding from that slight, dampened, decomposing ash.
Her voice stilled. One ruddy robin in the grass, dipping.

***Kene*: Bald Eagle**

For Buddy Weso

"O day and night, but this is wondrous strange!"
-Horatio (*Hamlet)*

My grandmother said we travel to stars
when we die. This dawn a bonfire hisses
blue flames against banked snow
guiding Uncle's journey from life
into unknown sky. Clouds obscure
heaven's embers. Around us white pines
collect tears from the driving wind.

Across the Wolf River a faint cry
and someone says "*kene*" just as softly
so I barely pick out both the bird's sound
and the spoken Algonquin word
from the burning, breaking splinters
and explosion of popping orange sparks—
familiar fireplace sounds I recognize—

but just as quickly I doubt soft voices
until again, in full daylight, the sound "*kene*."

The Bear Emerges

The sky shudders with first
thunder of spring. Bears
shake themselves and rise
to the voice above
and together, bears and sky
make a new year begin.

In bed we hear the rumble,
distant, as we find again
under blankets and skins,
the deep-set thud of heartbeats.
All through the hard winter
we forgot about rain and lightning.
We were alone except for
a cardinal and a pine. Now

as the day comes to life
we think of bears awakened
to sky-drums and wild onions.
We think of their growls
and claws scraped over bark.
We open a window and wet air
breathes into the house. Again
we are alive, again we are all alive.

Kansas Grasslands

for William Stafford

Big bluestem around us quivers,
alive as horse manes seem alive in wind.
This is the grass Stafford wrote
as though it were "the sky" or "forever,"

only this grass changes colors, mauve
by the Wakarusa River, and yellow,

and by roadside the bleached fox-tail grass.
Grass seed bundles brush against sky,
their long-tied knots loose at last.

We track deer, not Oregon whales,
in these waves, but still we drown
under eight-foot stalks of bluestem.
Switchback grass, too, splays
fronds overhead, like eagle-feather fans.

This imperfect circle is Stafford's horizon,
a curved line to keep stars from spilling,
a line through air, a thatched edge—
the path he traveled both ways.

Flint Hills Twilight

How shadows loosen from sloughs
and rise like floodwater.
Cedars shift rust-green to black.

I cannot tell if I am alone
or maybe with you again
within this diminished light.

*

After another earth-quarter turns away—
this world's quirk of axis—
and the sky rearouses:

violet and cobalt, then indigo.

You could be visible
against the last brilliant sky.

*

Singers and drummers begin the victory song:
this day will not die. Blue enflames the ridgeline,
a shining serpent twisting and lasting, lasting.

Great space separates each breath.
I could be on the edge of hills.
You could be barely within sight.

*

Before final loss, the moon rises—
orange globe, an exaggerated parallax
of human seasons and repetitions,

as red-tails and voles rest motionless.
You could be in the shadows waiting
or hidden in yesterday's night.

Shara McCallum

Biographical Sketch

Shara McCallum was born in Kingston, Jamaica in 1972. She immigrated to the US with her mother's grandparents and three of her (six) sisters in 1981. Her father died that year and her mother joined them in the states a year later. She has lived in Miami, the Baltimore/Washington D.C. area, upstate New York, Memphis, and currently resides in central Pennsylvania. She is married and is the mother of two young girls, Rachel and Naomi, ages 2 and 1/2 years and 9 and 1/2 months at the time of this writing. Shara McCallum is the author of two books of poems from the University of Pittsburgh Press, *Song of Thieves* (2003) and *The Water Between Us* (1999, winner of the 1998 Agnes Lynch Starrett Poetry Prize). Originally from Jamaica, McCallum directs the Stadler Center for Poetry and teaches at Bucknell University. She is also on the faculty of the Stonecoast Low Residency MFA program. She lives in Pennsylvania with her family.

Multiple Faiths

I was raised in the presence of multiple faiths: my parent's Rastafarianism, my maternal grandmother's Catholicism, and my maternal grandfather's (himself half-Anglican, half-Jewish) agnosticism. In the year I turned nine, my family immigrated to the U.S. and my father died. As these kinds of events are apt to do, they shook the foundation of my belief in a God who is aware of and concerned about human suffering. I've never regained that footing. Still, as an adult I have continued to long for the aesthetic and spiritual meaning to our lives that a belief in some notion of God sometimes imparts. Attracted to Judaism since my teens, I converted in my late twenties. Two statements I wrote during that time speak to the role spirituality plays in my poetry.One: "God is the absence that is everywhere a presence." Two: "Poetry is the closest I come to prayer."

Teresa of Avila (1515-82)

When St. Teresa sings
the word blossoms
on her lips, the spine
of the world splinters
into song. When she moves
her hips, she is no saint
but a woman beneath
her cassock, orange as the stain
of the sun. She is not burlap
sacks chafing skin but silken
threads sewn whole.
St. Teresa is the breath
she speaks but
cannot understand:
notes that are sounds,
words divorced
from meaning, only the feeling
of the Latin vowel and consonant
opening and closing
against her throat, a bird fluttering
its wings inside her chest.
St. Teresa is her own redemption,
her body feeding the flock,
her tongue a wafer of its own.
The host, a consecration
of her light, her spirit
and flesh radiating
against the halls of the church,
illuminating its darkest holds.

Facing It

Always the same questions
of blood and bread breaking,
eaten in communion

with what we know—this chair,
the candle flickering.
With what we don't—the dark
outside the window, night
ashen like the voice of my hands.

If I could again be a child
at my mother's side,
I would believe in the stove,
the lit room; in her skirt
swishing against my face
as I crumpled the hem in my fist,
made my hand a flag to wave
my mother's love into my skin.

I once was lost
but now am found, she hummed.
And we were, she and I.
And I believed in the night
more fiercely, believed
in my mother, my hand wrapt
in her skirt, moving back and forth
across my face, her face, the face
of God, the face I loved.

What I'm Telling You

for Steven

is what I read last week:
that we are ashes of stellar death.

That we rise to grace, blaze a moment,
only to smolder in our body's own defeat.

That the end is brilliant, yes,
but also a flurry of light and rage.

That we, you and I,
will cease to exist.

And I will never know this world
as this I again,

will never hold your face in my palms
once the end begins.

Even if physicists are right
and we are particles of celestial dust,

what was, is,
all that will ever be.

Even if the religious too
sing the same tune

when they speak of a world, a God,
without beginning or end.

Reincarnation, life-everlasting—
call it whatever you will—

it will not change
the facts: we are ashes of stellar death.

And, in the end, wishing on shooting stars
is like pinning your hopes

on the last sound of the whistle
trailing off, last chord of the train

sparking on the tracks
then fading into the dark.

The Waves

We walk into rooms that wait for us to enter them.
We walk into waves that threaten to drown us.

But they don't. They fill us instead
with salt, sand, and their own light.

As a child, from a small boat, I watched my father
swim away ignoring my mother's pleas, her voice

sucked into the wind, my own no match
for the undertow or sharks I feared.

There are moments in a life
when everything comes apart, is ripped so clean

who you are is laid bare. My father returned to us
that day. But he was not the same man

I had seen enter those waves.

My Father's Words

Once I was alone
so my father came to me,
told me the meaning
of flowers that open
by day, close their petals
at night to hide their face
from true light, flowers
that cannot brave
their own darkness.

Once my father was a night
I mistook for salvation,
a voice I mistook for myself.

Once my father
was a bird with wings of longing
and despair, a field of words
blossoming in my ear,
telling me: *my child,*
this is all there is.

The News

Nothing falls from the sky to claim me.
These days, I am a bird with stones
in its beak, warbling an awful tune.

The news from beyond reaches me
always too late. What girl has fallen now,
off what coast, into what ocean or sea?

Wasn't the water already filling with blood?
Hasn't it always been so?
These days, I exchange the world

outside my window for one within. I close
my ears to that girl's final cries, listening
instead to my own child, singing at play.

Somewhere a mother is facing a truth
she will have to rehearse daily to believe.
While the news clatters on,

the hem of her life will be snagged,
from here forward, in the moment a child
can't find her way back home.

For Rachel, Just before Speech

We are the body moving toward demise;
we are the *soul*, remnant of another life.

And always, rain tapping on a zinc roof
is the sound of fingers, thrumming flesh.

Always, I return
to the things of this world, tethered.

You, who have come to me
from something, somewhere, I cannot name;

you who have a voice that does not speak
any language I know, yet unfurls its wings,

alighting in each corner of this house;
you who are mine and not mine,

tell me the answers
while there is time.

Alicia Ostriker

Biographical Sketch

Alicia Suskin Ostriker (November 11, 1937) was born in Brooklyn, New York to David and Beatrice Linnick Suskin. Her mother read her Shakespeare, and Alicia began writing poems at an early age. Ostriker holds a bachelor's degree from Brandeis University , and an M.A. and Ph.D. from the University of Wisconsin. Her doctoral dissertation, on the work of William Blake, became her first book, *Vision and Verse in William Blake* (1965). She began her teaching career at Rutgers University in 1965 and has served as a professor of English there since 1972.

Alicia Ostriker, twice a finalist for the National Book Award, has published eleven volumes of poetry, most recently *No Heaven*. Her most recent prose book is *Dancing at the Devil's Party: Essays on Poetry, Politics, and the Erotic*. Ostriker lives in Princeton, NJ, and teaches in the low-residency Poetry MFA program of New England College.

Poetry as a Spiritual Practice

Raised by atheist parents, I've always been drawn to the poetry of the sacred. Whitman and Blake are my great heterodox visionary heroes. They speak to my experience of reality. As someone who has never been able to feel comfortable with any kind of organized religion, I've always seen my poetry as my spiritual practice. Sometimes the spiritual dimension is less obvious, sometimes more so. To me it is always clear: spiritual quest is what my work is about. Since the mid-eighties, I've also written consciously as a Jew, but a Jew who wrestles with God, with my tradition, and with other Jews. My "psalms" are in a sense anti-psalms since they would never be accepted by the Orthodox.

Dear God

It used to be
I would fall to the floor and press my forehead to it
In moments of despair

I would say help me
Help me

But listen
I am ok
But I just now found myself pressing my forehead
To the carpet of my stairs

About the waters in flooded New Orleans
Poisoned by oilspill, chemicals, the dead
About the survivors forever traumatized
Dear god
I am alive I am alive
Help them

Approaching Seventy

Sit and watch the memory disappear
Romance disappear the probability
Of new adventures disappear

Well isn't it beautiful
When the sun goes down
Don't we all want to be where we can watch it

Redden
Sink to a spark
Disappear

*

Your friend goes to Sri Lanka and works
For a human rights organization
In the middle of a civil war

Where she too might be disappeared any time
And another friend goes to retreats
Sits miserably waiting for ecstasy and ecstasy

Actually comes, so many others
So many serial monogamists seeking love
Some open doorway some wild furious breath

*

Please, I thought, when I first saw the paintings
De Kooning did when Alzheimer's had taken him
Into its arms and he could do nothing

But paint, purely paint, transparent, please let me
Make beauty like that, sometime, like an infant
That can only cry,

And suckle, and shit, and sleep,
Boneless, unaware, happy,
Brush in hand no ego there he went

*

A field of cerise another of lime
A big curve slashes across canvas
Then another there it is the lucidity

Each of us longs for
As if everything belonging to the other world
That we forget at birth is finally flooding

Back to the man like a cold hissing tide
Wave after wave where he waits on the shore
Of the canvas brush in hand

*

So give it up, lady, get yourself over
To the sandy shore with the sleeping gulls
—Does the tide rise or doesn't it

And are you or are you not willing
To rise from sleep, yes, in the dark, and patiently
Go outside and wait for it

And do you know what is meant by patience
Do you know what is meant by going outside
Do you know what is meant by the tide

Four Psalms from *the volcano sequence, 2002*

Psalm

I am not lyric any more
I will not play the harp
for your pleasure

I will not make a joyful
noise to you, neither
will I lament

for I know you drink
lamentation, too,
like wine

so I dully repeat
you hurt me
I hate you

I pull my eyes away from the hills
I will not kill for you
I will never love you again

unless you ask me

Psalm

I endure impure periods
when I cannot touch you

or even look at you
you are a storm I would be electrocuted

by your approach then I feel some sort of angelic laughter
like children behind a curtain

come, I think
you are at my fingertips my womb

you are the wild driver of my vehicle
the argument in my poem

nothing between us
only breath

Psalm

my head is uncovered to my naked hair
I am dressed immodestly

my old body lacks teeth, lacks a breast
still cherishes itself

I eat what I want I am
an animal of flesh

as you know for you formed me in the womb
and made my desires what they are

I am waiting for you
in a bed of pleasure

Psalm

like a skin on milk
I write to you

I hurl the letters of your name
onto every page, one and many

I know you are reading over my shoulder
look each of us possesses a book of life

each attempts to read what the other has scripted
in these almost illegible letters tipped by crowns

what is the story
we want to know

Everywoman Her Own Theology

I am nailing them up to the cathedral door
Like Martin Luther. Actually, no,
I don't want to resemble that *Schmutzkopf*
(See Erik Erikson and N. 0. Brown
On the Refortner's anal aberrations,
Not to mention his hatred of Jews and peasants),
So I am thumbtacking these ninety-five
Theses to the bulletin board in my kitchen.

Mv proposals, or should I say requirements,
Include at least one image of a god,
Virile, beard optional, one of a goddess,
Nubile, breast size approximating mine,
One divine baby, one lion, one lamb,
All nude as figs, all dancing wildly,
All dancing. Reproducible
In marble, metal, in fact any material.

Ethically, I am looking for
An absolute endorsement of loving-kindness.

No loopholes except maybe mosquitoes.
Virtue and sin will henceforth be discouraged,
Along with suffering and martyrdom.
There will be no concept of infidels;
Consequently the faithful must entertain
Themselves some other way than killing infidels.

And so forth and so on. I understand
This piece of paper is going to be
Spattered with wine one night at a party
And covered over with newer pieces of paper.
That is how it goes with bulletin boards.
Nevertheless it will be there.
Like an invitation, like a chalk pentangle,
It will emanate certain occult vibrations.

If something sacred wants to swoop from the universe
Through a ceiling, and materialize,
Folding its silver wings,
In a kitchen, and bump its chest against mine,
My paper will tell this being where to find me.

Eric Pankey

Biographical Sketch

Eric Pankey was born in Kansas City in 1959, the youngest of three children. He attended public schools in Raytown, Missouri, and continued his education at the University of Missouri and the University of Iowa. His parents, both bookkeepers, took his bookishness in stride and encouraged his interest in written and visual arts. He and his wife, the poet Jennifer Atkinson, live in Fairfax, Virginia. They have one daughter, Clare, who attends Elon University.

Eric Pankey is the author of seven collections of poems, most recently *Oracle Figures* and *Reliquaries*, both from Ausable Press. Professor of English and Heritage Chair in Writing at George Mason University, he has received fellowships from the Ingram Merrill Foundation, The National Endowment for the Arts, and the John Simon Guggenheim Foundation.

The Word

The Word is and without advent. As a body is a grave, so too is a word.

Do we through words remove ourselves from, or attach ourselves to the otherness we name?

The given, often in these discussion, is that we live in an era *after* belief— the god's death not as yet another myth about the god, but historical fact. I am not sure I begin at the given. After the death of god, the god goes on living as god, called forth as before by words.

Words no not veil but reveal. Words do not reveal but veil.

In the beginning was the Word, and all the following words are embellishments upon the Word,

In the beginning was the Word, and all the following words are splinters from the Word.

Some poets want words to be transparent, to illuminate. Some poets want words to be impenetrable, to obscure. Many believers approach the Word in the same way.

We know the world as a translation.

Detail from "The Lamentation over the Dead Christ"

The final gift that each affords
Is grief— requisite, not kindred—
A dismal freight as dense as gold.

As a body borne to its tomb
Is carried, so too they lift
Their pain and leave it here with him.

It weighs upon him like a cloth
Infused in oils and spices,
A rancid balm bitter with ruth.

But she holds him as in her womb.
Now dread, not wonder, tinctures awe.
Once. Once she was alive with him.

Homage

1.
O my God, looming and rough-hewn,
Forge me with rage. If this is the purge
Ferret out and scald the cold grub
Burrowed in at my heart. Let havoc
Consume its nest and larder.
Let you gold cauter stanch the wound.

2.
Fall inviolate sledge, and be known.
Blast away the sawdust and matchwood,
The ash-fall and rusted filings.
Let me be your wedge, let that edge
Gleam from use, burnished as it divides
The flawed from this hammerdressed world.

Palm Sunday

Three weeks ago forsythia rattled its sticks.
Now, though not an answer, not a reprieve,
The redbud flowers from it hard black trunk
And the magnolia rocks in the wind,

An ark that carries only whiteness and blush.
The dogwood's limbs have not revealed their bracts'
Stigmata, and for that she is thankful.
Why does He descend into the city,

She wonders each year, into History,
His advance raising up dust, a figure
Of dust, which is each of us following
Him? Dust the wind easily disperses?

And why do we repeat the meager fanfare,
The palm leaves bidding welcome and farewell?
She descends the church stairs and does what she must.
She hurries home to the life that's hers.

Each year she looks out for an answer and finds
Only spring's unmiraculous onslaught.

In Memory

If the world is create from the Word,
What will I hear amid the noise of that one
Assertion and all that rattles and diminishes

In its wake: the mockingbird's trill and grate,
The sluice and overlap where the creek narrows,
The dragonfly needling through the humid air?

And what will I hear when words are no more?
I cannot hear you know, ash-that-you-are,
My beloved, who in your passion and error,

In what was your life gave life to me,
My life from the life of your blunt body
That is no more. If I believe that Christ

Is risen, why can't I believe that we too
Will be risen, rejoined, and relieved
Of the world's tug and the body's ballast?

We are asked to testify, to bear
Witness to what we have seen and heard,
And yet our hope is in the veiled and silenced.

I take comfort in your silence,
In the absence of the voice that voiced your pain.
The body apart from the spirit is dead

But that does not mean the spirit is dead.

My Mother Amid the Shades

If you are my son, what proof do you offer?
I give you the annunciatory angel's lily.
I give you the rubric of Christ's hidden scripture.

If you are my son, these are not yours to offer.
I give you a wine bowl of ivy wood,
I give you four walls of wild pear, a roof of gold.

If you are my son, what proof do you offer?
I give you a field of windfall ripe with wasps.
I give you a single pear wrapped in tissue.

If you are my son, these are not yours to offer.
I give you the story of my father, your husband.
I give you all that was taken from him.

If you are my son, what proof do you offer?
None. The pyre, at last, translated all to ash.
At the border, they took everything his name.

History

A hundred flint arrowheads, chipped, rain-washed, scattered through a meadow of ragweed and clover,
The flesh they ripped, the rib nicked, the shields of horsehide torn, all lost to the elements;
An ice-pierced daybreak through a mica screen and the first lute arrives in China from Persia;

The uses of ambergris are perfected; the lamb's blood dries above the doorway; a glacier calves an iceberg;
From the rock where a father offered up his son as sacrifice, the Prophet ascends into paradise;
The summer you step on a rusted nail, the willows green and bend to the river; the river floods;

Before nightfall, a body is bargained for, secreted away in a borrowed grave fashioned from a cave;
Again, walls and towers topple. And no language but grief is left in common. And grief no language at all.
There is no history, only fits and starts, laughter at the table, lovers asleep, slaughter, the forgetfulness,

And yet for three nights straight, nothing but starlight— Byzantine, quicksilver, an emanation of a past—
And tonight you have renamed the constellations after the mudras: *The Gesture Beyond Mercy,*
The Gesture for Warding Off Evil, The Gesture of Fearlessness, The Gift-Bestowing Gesture of Compassion. .

Let Me Rest upon that Peaceful Mountain

Soon enough I will wash my hands above the spoils, soon enough feat among the flies
At a table, daubed and speckled, where my ghost will sit before the body it once burdened.
Until then, I transcribe the changes: salt into air, air into anthracite, anthracite into fern.
Until then, I watch the creek shrink and fill through the seasons.
I watch the moon, cloaked in camouflage, lift like a zeppelin.

*

"Those old songs are my lexicon and prayer book," Dylan says of "I Saw the Light,"
"Let Me Rest on that Peaceful Mountain," and "Keep on the Sunny Side."
I put on Neil Young's "Only Love Can Break Your Heart," Tom Waits' "Jesus Gonna Be Here"
And "The Cold, Cold Ground,"
and Emmylou Harris's cover of Lucinda Williams' "Sweet Old World."
What comfort I fell, though broken and buried, at the promise of redemption on this passing earth.

*

More and more I forget the names of things or I'll step into a room and forget my I entered.
If I wait, what has slipped catches up with me, the name or reason, and I go about my business.
Every day at 5:05 someone calls, and when I pick up the phone, the person says nothing.
Hello, I say once or twice, then we listen to one another breathe and neither of us wants to be the first
To hang up, to be the one to let the other have such a sublime, mischievous, and useless satisfaction.

*

A hawk settled and preened on a low-branched oak outside the church
window.
I was impatience at that very moment with questions of the spirit.
Pure in its severity, the hawk turned its head, and though I saw its eyes, I
did not meet them.
Beyond these wooded acres:
the Little River Turnpike, the road home.
How often the *out-there* seems a diorama, a lesson in an enclosure, an
example of the real.

Tim Seibles

Biographical Sketch

Tim Seibles was born in Philadelphia, Pennsylvania in 1955. He is the author of several books of poems including *Hurdy-Gurdy*, *Hammerlock* and, most recently, *Buffalo Head Solos*—each published by the Cleveland State University Poetry Center Press. He is a former National Endowment for the Arts fellow and has been a writing fellow at the Provincetown Fine Arts Work Center in Massachusetts. He also received an Open Voice Award from the 63rd Street Y in New York City. His work has been featured in anthologies such as *Humor Me*, *Role Call*, *Outsiders*, and *The Poets' Grimm*. He has been a workshop leader for Cave Canem—a retreat for African American writers—and for the Zora Neale Hurston-Richard Wright Foundation. He lives in Norfolk, Virginia, where he is a member of Old Dominion University's English Department and MFA in Writing faculty.

Engine of the Divine

Perhaps Spirit is the engine of a life, an appetite that moves each of us around in the world—asking us to see more, feel more deeply, be more thoroughly conscious, compassionate. I don't know. In fact, insofar as Spirit is an emblem of The Divine, much of its sweet power is in its mystery. What I hope is that my poems—whether I'm singing to The Goddess or not—are visible signs of my struggle to awaken, to challenge and move beyond the generally accepted, dull-eyed notions of what it means to be Here. For me, that is the quintessential spiritual task, and poetry is the means by which I bear witness to it.

In a Glance

I'm caught in this curling energy! Your hair!
Whoever's calm and sensible is insane!
- Rumi

The unseeable   seen!—that saxophone
spilling from the window—a true very soon

held between two lips: Her smile   for no reason
a carnival quietly placed   a flaze
made to bathe in   the right door gliding
belightedly up the boulevard:

All day my heart face-down my pulse
pecking like a chickadee sick of its
short wings I had hoped some astonishing

would scratch the gravel from my eyes:
sunset hatched from a soup can   a tree toad
tap-dancing with a tadpole… Perhaps
a meat flag   fricasseed above

my dumb country   but never the burning wheel
of a slow hour: Her smile   a glass blown yes
two maybes dressed in a wish—   three buttercups

in a jade vase under a blue umbrella

a cello ablaze with me drawing myself
along the strings her smile plays:

To feel so much! But not go mad enough
to shuck the grave in my skull. To scrub
and bumble for the glum Puppeteer

while my heart my teeth my
orthopedic verbs strain
like mice in a scrum
My voice! Bruised and shoeless

goes mumbling the streets
trying to buy a vowel

My alphabet used to be 10 feet long—
every letter a xylophone a shark's leg a
flubber ballooning my whole soul a holler
from the blind church of the unsaid: *Her smile*,

sly melody glad enough to fling the grass afire
kind season that rings the light beyond Her lips:

But soft! Me, a man collided, the both the between—

the lovely shape of a mind unshaved by reason—
Over the over   banging into the change

Ambition

III Primate, Bipedal

This: to find no distance
between what I am and what I seem.
To catch myself between myself

and the mirror   unafraid,
afraid of everything, *everything*.
To not have History
Scaling my face.

To break the thumbs
that hung the world. To tear those hands
with these dull teeth. Human

almost. To hate. To reason. To burn,
while the Sphinx feathers my ear

saying, saying *who   are you   talking to?*

This: to be pure

animal—my blood
unlocked, my legs

scribbled with hair, my soul
perched on my shoulder. Free.
Unconvinced   of my name: on my tongue,

for the first time, salt.

To chase this   then *be* this,
then sleep. This. I want *this*
to be my life: to come back

with a mouth ready
to send new noise.
To learn again

how to stand, how to put one foot
down   then the other a little farther along.

Late Shift

Places—
maybe dreams

from which I cannot   return: the velvet

touch of Her lips, first light
fingering a cup: sacred dislocations

of mind—the way the right sound
becomes visible.

Where I am now
it's later—the clocks have been amended

to include all the strange hours—
and Someone cracked my name

as if all my life I'd been locked inside.

I know the shelves stay stocked, big cars lead the chase,
there's always more   and more to eat.

But was that ever   my country?

I was.   born there.
And I'd go back   if I could—

just to feel less lonely—
but what I took

to be a certain distance

was actually a late   shift in myself,

a different kind of listening:
the voice, a thread of honey—

the jar tipped   just enough to one side:

Listen.

We belong to no nation.

One day we will hold the Earth
again   as if She were a love

nearly lost, Her rainy hair tangled in our hands.

The soul is what we are.
Every life   a word the wind turns to say.

And though trouble grows back like a beard,
an unchained blood governs my tongue.

I have seen the door   that is not there

still open

Anthem

for Aditi

I would have a new name—
all vowels and two m's
to which I would come
when You called. No, no word

but a stitch of wind,
a light come-hither
in the billowing trees, the fizz
of fresh ginger-ale: that

would be my name.
A trellis of nothing
but shadow, a cup
of smoke, the glare
of something broken,

call me *that*,
and I will arrive
like a season the size
of a hand, like the smell
of hot soup, I will be
Where You are—

my shoes empty,
my voice knocked
sideways, my tongue
buttoned all wrong
like a little boy's shirt.

Woman, I'll never find my name,
nor an anthem for this
starved country in my chest,

but if that *might*   bring me
the taste of Your mouth
I will keep trying to sing

because this near music, this
time spent drowning, this one
small shining amidst all the worry
is still paradise. I swear

on the blood of my soul
I've seen the proof: a good world

spoken twice in Your dark eyes

and the perfect democracy
of sky   spilling over

the citizens and the shape
of Your lips   and Your smile

which must be my lost name.

Ravi Shankar

Biographical Sketch

Ravi Shankar was born in Washington DC and lived his childhood in Manassas, VA, known for the Battles of Bull Run and Lorena Bobbitt, and in Coimbatore, South India. He has worked at a variety of jobs including as a knife salesmen, a dry wall hanger, a mixologist and a soccer referee. He now resides on the banks of the Connecticut River in the quintessentially New England village town of Chester, CT, where he might just represent the town's entire population of color.

Poet-in-residence at Central Connecticut State and founding editor of *Drunken Boat*, Ravi Shankar has published, *Instrumentality* (Cherry Grove), a book of poems named a finalist for the 2005 Connecticut Book Awards. He has appeared as a commentator on NPR, written poems, reviews and essays for such publications as *The Paris Review, Fulcrum, Time Out New York* and *Poets & Writers*, and read his work in many venues, including the Asia Society, Columbia University, and the National Arts Club. Along with Tina Chang and Nathalie Handal, he is currently editing an anthology of contemporary Arab and Asian poetry, due out from Norton in fall 2007.

Language & Spirituality

Language, which predates and will outlast us, postulates a certain utility, in pointing at things in the world, in conjuring through rhetoric points of view, in describing human relations and natural phenomenon with commensurate measures of sublimity, but what it can also do, under the pressure of intense perception, or alternately the flitting of unexpected revelation, is create a bridge between the known and the unknown, between the edible and the indelible, or as W. B. Yeats would have it, between self and soul. Such poems, when they arrive, are distilled communications from the ether that allow us to better understand our natures and the reality in which we find ourselves. In contracting the cosmic mysteries into the dense, sprung lyricism of a poem, words find their true shape, and though born from air and nothingness, like humans, they can impart timeless wisdom, searing accusations, transcendent epiphanies, and plaintive song to whoever encounters them. Such words achieve the permanence of a star or pebble, no less profound for being completely illusory. My poems, in some small way, hope to partake in that dialogue and further the exploration of consciousness into itself and so beyond.

One Stone to Samadhi

Back in the room, it's as if we never left:
A cone of frangipani gradually charring,
And *Clair de Lune*, overlaid with whale song,

Piping through tweeters in the background,
Plastic folding-chairs filled with disparate frames
In similar postures: back straight, palms open

Upon thighs, eyes closed, muscles relaxed,
The flicker of thought, in principle, sacrificed
To the rising and falling of breath. Still a fleck

Of peripheral self can't help but remain, temporarily
Unhooked from memory's flux and grapple,
Yet attendant in some form nonetheless,

A watchfulness impartial to inclination,
Though to speak of it is like pointing a finger
At the moon. Suffice it to say that, eyes closed,

The crest on passing time's ongoing wave
Perpetually furnishes the mind with vista,
And back in the room, it's as if we never arrived.

Peacock

Upon a corbelled stone wall, a thrall of eyes
peers from a train draped iridescent across
mid-afternoon, embroidered from Saturn's

rings perhaps, lustrous with crescent sheen,
burning bright blue and green like a dare
not to take seriously the premise of intelligent

design. How feathered audacity weighs
proportionally more than a bejeweled crown

upon a king's bald pate. What roving beak

knows it's festooned with a drum major's tom,
imperial and startling. When an ostentation
of birds constitutes an aesthetic unarguable.

Clouds

Earth-breath: parcels of air inhaling
water vapor from thermal currents,
seas, groundswells, breathing out

in wisps and pillars barrier from deep
space or direct sun. Light as froth,
else mean, pure tumult to a pilot,

polluted air rife with nuclei for rain-
drops to form on, ink-dark filaments
a portent poised to squall and roar.

Up here, above them, rolling tufts
subdividing sky and sky, perpetual
motion feels Eleatic. Motionless.

Shaking Free of Epiphany

Remember that voice which briefly nested
In your friend's mouth as you both stood
On a mountaintop fringed with trillium

Wondering what to do with the rest of life,
A runnel of wind winding through the trees?
Remember how the voice, which was not

Quite your friend's voice, being somehow
Deeper, more pronounced and bell-like,
Bypassed the usual interpretive mechanisms,

Spoke directly to your constitutional core?
Remember the memories that surged up then,
Of being a child in a clearing gazing at stars

Bare arms infused with the crispness of grass,
The steady whine of crickets scoring the dark,
Every element, including yourself, pristine?

That was when, though later you'd disavow it,
Tears came, along with a need for something
You might, if you weren't so modern, call

Redemption, a poignant awareness of how
Far from the child you'd been you'd come
And how much farther there was to go,

The only guide to what lay ahead threadbare
Words that had been spoken too many times
By too many people to hold significance.

Where on the horizon were the new words,
The ones the size of pills, the color of plums,
Sharpened and stainless as geometric forms,

The words that curled the toes in convulsion,
Stole behind the barn with a can of gasoline
And lit a match, danced round the flames

So as to summon drought from the rains?
Where were the words that would transform
Facsimile folk, turning slurs pure as spring

Water, saturating pores of Diaspora,
Words that would partake equally of neon
And oak leaf, timeless yet encompassing

The prefixes neo-, hyper-, cyber- and post-,
Where on the tip of your tongue were they?
The wind then, not in response, eddied

Through the green scrim of birch and ash,
And a white-tailed deer sprang in front of you,
Rubbing its nose against the ground, casting,

If demeanor can be imputed to animals,
A prolonged, quizzical glance at the two of you
Before bounding into the leaf-heavy beyond.

When you turned to your friend to confirm
The passing creature, no sounds would come
From your mouth, though ideas teemed;

Somehow the self at the helm of the larynx
Was estranged from the one picking wordless
Fruit on the shores of intention. A disconnect.

Have you forgotten what happened next,
How in your friend's eyes, which until now
Had resembled noon-light refracted through

A magnifying glass, personality was restored,
The bell-like voice replaced by familiar
Intonations, the parasite returned to its host?

How you put your arms around each other
As if having survived an infantry's final burst?
How the clear skies broke into storm,

A hard rain buffeting briefly then dying out?
The car ride down the mountain was filled
With silence, both of you turning over coins

Of thought minted in different countries,
Unable to explain to each other a hairline
Fracture appearing in your sense of things,

An imperative indelibly etched on any plans
You might make in the near or far,
And so you listened instead to indie rock

Crackling through the car speakers, watched
The onset of evening through the windshield,
Patches of mailbox-fronted homes scrolling past.

That night, alone, the blue light of television
Could not diminish your neural circuitry's buzz,
Your palpable certainty that ontological

Change was fermenting in your chest, that
You could engage the real as the deer did,
Regal and unwavering in pursuit of finality.

That night you dreamed of a black hull nudging
Past silt and reeds, opening into an expanse
Of flawless rippling ocean, interstitial spaces

Shifting while maintaining a pattern between
The wingtips of gulls wheeling in formation
Overhead, skies roughly the color of the sea,

A gray blanket of serenity that swaddled you . . .
If only morning hadn't come, but it did,
Refastening hasps on an extant worldview,

The thought processes which conveyed you
From fast-food lunches to movie houses,
From facing mirrors to the back of bars,

Though you were never quite able to forget
What transpired that day on the mountaintop.
O parched, membranous glutton! How many

Years have passed since you first saw the light
Gleaming from the mask of your friend's face
Who is now married, expecting a third child?

How many years paralyzed, unable to decipher,
Have you tried to love someone who loves you
But found it nearly impossible to do so?

"You remember too much," a toothless sibyl
Diagnosed, "your corolla has been tinged black
By a curse put on you in some former life."

She gave you crystals to dissolve in a hot bath,
Lotion made from an extract of bergamot
And vetiver root, three beeswax candles to light

At the stroke of midnight, but it hasn't helped,
Has it? My advice to you—beware, it's biased—
Is to sit on a mat that vibrates at eight thousand

Angstroms and concentrate on a plastic ashtray,
Lime-green and perfect in its Platonic oval,
And if that fails, to pick up a pencil and write.

Vivian Shipley

Biographical Sketch

Vivian Shipley was raised in Kentucky and has spent the last forty years in Connecticut which she now calls her second home. She is the Connecticut State University Distinguished Professor and Editor of *Connecticut Review* from Southern Connecticut State University. Shipley has published five chapbooks and her seventh book of poems, *Hardboot: Poems New & Old*, (Southeastern Louisiana University Press, 2005) won the 2006 Paterson Prize for Sustained Literary Achievement. She won the 2005 Lifetime Achievement Award for Service to the Literary Community from the Library of Congress Connecticut Center for the Book and the 2005 SCSU Faculty Scholar Award. *Gleanings: Old Poems, New Poems* (Southeastern Louisiana University Press, 2003) was nominated for the Pulitzer Prize. *When There Is No Shore*, also nominated for the Pulitzer Prize, won the 2003 Connecticut Book Award for Poetry from the Library of Congress' Center for the Book and the 2002 Word Press Poetry Prize. She has won numerous awards for her poetry including the Ann Stanford Poetry Prize from University of Southern California and the Hart Crane Poetry Prize from Kent State University.

Spirituality

A priest is blessed to be able to offer a communion wafer that provides salvation to a deeply troubled world. Poets have only their words to give. Many of my poems are meant to be prayers, offering the solace one who believes might find in prayer. What I do believe is that evil in this world will not be tamed, that widespread injustice will not be curbed. But

I bear witness and write to record the struggle of the heart, the mind, the body ensnared by powers that cannot be understood or controlled. I believe that what we have is here and now, the world with its terrifying power to destroy or to enchant with its beauty and wonders.

At the center of every religion is a longing for permanence, for an answer to what lies beyond death in order to justify suffering on this earth. When I was 30 and pregnant with my second son, I had seizures and was taken to the hospital where labor was induced. Todd was born and doctors discovered a brain tumor in my right frontal lobe that was almost the size of a small grapefruit. I was given a 10% chance of surviving surgery. Even as the anesthesia dripped into me, I could not pray. After I recovered, I felt the need to preserve my spirit not in an afterlife but in the present one. For the first time, I began to write poetry, perhaps in an attempt to understand my months of meaningless physical pain, to translate the terrible thing that had happened into something positive. Having a brain tumor caused me to become a poet and now it is often the bad fortune that happens to others which is not linked to any apparent reason that prompts me to write. My finger on the edge of an acrylic plate put in by the surgeon to replace my skull is a constant reminder of the fragility of life. As a consequence, many of my poems struggle with the question of why some voices are silenced and why others surface. Why is one person victim to a suicide bomber and not another? It is easy to take gifts of health, love, happiness for granted until they are taken like the ground during an earthquake.

I was raised as a Methodist with a very fundamental faith which I have lost even though I yearn for the certainty of my early religious experience. I am not sure of what happens to the spirit after death, but I do know that each day is what we have and that each day contains grace if we seek to find what is sacred. When I moved my parents from Kentucky to Connecticut to care for them because my father was dying of cancer, I had to take them from the house that my father had built. My mother and father knew they would never return to their beloved home. Before leaving, I dug up box after box of peony tubers from their side yard and brought them to Connecticut. The peonies had come from my grandmother's farm outside of Somerset, Kentucky and Grandma Todd had taken them from her mother's Pulaski County farm. Today, I raked leaves and unearthed maroon leaves starting to sprout from tubers that had rooted in three generations of Kentucky earth. I thought of the beauty, the ravishing pink, white and fuscia flowers of the peony brought the spirits of my parents, my grandparents and my great-parents back to me, back into this world.

Nourishing to my heart like the peonies, writing my poems is a quest I undertake each day to find some meaning for an individual life. The spiritual journey is universal unlike the physical one of the body which is personal. Poetry can ease the quest, the journey because when words are placed on a page, are given the permanence of print, the spirit has prevailed, will endure.

Survivors Have Victims

We turn from what destroys us, in time if we can,
and gather what can be held: my grandmother's plate
of full-blown yellow and pink roses scalloped in gold.

Coming back to take what was left of my mother's cherry
chest after the tornado outside Somerset, we found drawers
strewn on the foundation as if a thief, finding no money

or jewelry, was goaded to anger. Devil's Lane was where
we walked that summer my grandfather's farm was leveled,
the cows sucked out as barns flew apart, boards lifting

like souls going to heaven in Raphael's Transfiguration.
Clover, there was clover everywhere we stepped. I tied stem
to flower to double wreath my wrist which had no tattooed

numbers you could recite from your father's arm. Comparing
our love to Kentucky's Natural Bridge we crossed the day
after our wedding, you predicted we would leapfrog old laws

that forbid the marriage of Gentile and Jew. Picturing gloves
made from baby skin in an Israeli museum, you translated
Buchenwald and Belsen into medical grand rounds for me:

experimenting with labor, women's feet were not raised
like a mare's are in a blacksmith's shop, but thighs strapped
together. With no exit, life could not peel from its core.

Strung together, your words couldn't metaphor those mothers,
wombs sealed into a mausoleum. Of course I felt ethical rage,
but there was no common ground in the miles separating us,

Germany to Africa to Kentucky. I mouthed genocide, holocaust
to meet the challenge of understanding years I could not pull
myself through. When I saw you holding breath in our shower,

I knew you were testing how long you would last if the water
stopped. In time, there were fences between us that kept rising
like hot air, like the gas none of my family had ever inhaled.

Knowing what cannot be swallowed must be spit out or it will
rot like strings of beans caught between teeth, I choked on soil
planted with your deaths. I couldn't blanket your grandparents'

shadows, could not pull three sons away in time from our flames.
When they smoldered, you fanned them, needing to keep anger
burning, burning through years that can never be consumed.

When Your Number's Up

Rocking on the front porch with eyes closed to feel late sun,
my grandmother preached to her congregation
of dogs, cats, chickens, The hairs of your head are numbered.
I pictured her hands, fingers layered between
knuckles, and thumbs twiddling like blades of a reel mower

cutting hay, as a barber shaved my head with an electric razor.
Piling around me like stacks of wheat
before it is gathered and tied in Brueghel's The Harvesters,
my hair was red then gold in the air
as it dropped. Way too pretty to throw away, the orderly

said as he gathered it in a sack for me to keep. The night
before the meningioma was removed,
I had to translate the medical word for brain tumor to my kin
as they circled around me. Holding
hands while they sang hymns, their trust was in the mighty

fortress of god not the surgeon. Folding my fingers into
my palms, index fingers and thumbs pointed to
heaven, I used to play Here's the church, here's the steeple.
Open the doors and here's the people.
During the operation, my hands were strapped down.

I couldn't pray without them. I lived. I could add. Emptying
the bag I brought from Gaylord Hospital, I counted
each strand of hair on my bed, told myself: Hustle! Ink
your lucky number on an arm, go to Lighthouse Deli,
buy a fistful of Quik Pic, Daily Lotto, Play Four and Power Ball.

A Keeper

If it's warm and windless on Long Island Sound, if the tide
turns late in the morning, if high clouds block the sun,
we'll leave Longshore Boat Basin in Westport and head

across the flats inside of Seymour's Rock. We'll catch
the best of the rip on the backside of Cockenoe. Past
the tip of Saugatuck Shores, there will be a swirl,

a gull swooping to pick at bait and that will be our signal
to swing close, cut the engine and drift. First, we'll try
a Fiord spoon next to the grass, alternate pulling

and dragging as we reel in. If we get a hit, a surging run,
we may not have a bluefish. If as we work it to the side,
we see bronze stripes gleaming, we'll know it's a bass.

If it measures thirty four inches or more, we'll have
a keeper. Then we can settle back, drink a Samuel Adams
while I tell you how my father used a croppie killer

and rooster tail for lures. In Carr Creek, Kentucky,
he was baptized with a napkin tied over his hair
which the preacher blessed during the minute of total

emersion. For the rest of his life, my father used
that head rag to wipe his lures for luck so God would
be with him. He swore on the family Bible that he once

caught a gar so big that when it took off swimming,
the bottom burst right out of the boat. If we haven't run
out of tide before we've run out of beer, we'll head around

for Cockenoe's southwest corner, passing clumps of reeds
midway across the west side. Maybe there will be
a fly-rodder standing in an aluminum boat. Maybe

blackfish will swirl just as we reach the tide rip. The drift
might carry us out across the rip, around the backside
of the island. We could try a popper on a spinning rod

if our arms have not had enough, if we have more
than stories about the thirty three inch blue or
the thirty two inch striper we threw back. So we can

make sense of how we spent the day, we need more
than just our arms spread apart estimating the size to take
back for our daughters. We need more than faith, we need

a blue we can fillet on the kitchen counter, one we can
hold like the head rag my father twisted in his hands,
a keeper that we can mount to hang above the fireplace.

I Have Come to Witness the Sacred

Like conch shells washed ashore, the wild horses
of Corolla brought to Florida by Ponce De Leon

in 1526 are gifts to Outer Banks, to North Carolina.
I'm certain they'll be lean, sleeker than Indian ponies,

skim sand, kick foam to lace. No J. Alfred Prufrock,
wild horses will be sacred as mermaids, will sing to me,

Combing the white hair of the waves blown back.
It's only three hours north from here in Ocracoke

to Corolla's Currituck Lighthouse where I should find
them, free as cattle in New Delhi. No time for flight,

I bypass Nags Head, Kitty Hawk, 1900: hang gliders,
Dayton, Ohio bicycle builders, Wright brothers

bumping, stumbling, floating for seconds of glory. I do
stop at Duck to check in at the Sanderling. Its beaches

are glutted by mollusk, but there's no smell of chorine,
only Coppertone from children uncaged by their parents

who lounge like buffet silverware. Too much life is left
on these shores to thicken and clot like Jack Daniel's gravy

that is not stirred. I need the sacred, the wild horses
of Corolla, to be rinsed clean like Lewis and Clark portaging

dugout canoes at Great Falls in order to reach headwaters
of the Missouri River. No promontory like Cape Hatteras,

Currituck Lighthouse is surrounded by lawn of County Cork,
glowing but not green as bluegrass fencing Kentucky stallions

on Calumet Farms. My quest for the Holy Grail ends.
One head pokes out between white framed houses. Two,

five, finally six horses laze over the street. Short and portly,
with an air of salmon fed bankers, that last one must be

sleep walking. In conference about browsing, dumpy, trash
can clanging, shambling pests are the star I have followed.

Elizabeth Anne Socolow

Biographical Sketch

Liz Socolow grew up with dogs and the sound of tugboats in her sleep near the East River in Manhattan, after a a brief two years in the shadow of the Bronx Botanical Garden, to which she attributes her passion for ferns, especially, and more generally raising plants and gardening. She currently lives with some hundred pots of green beings in New Jersey near one grown sun and his family; she invades the San Francisco Garden of her other son and his wife. She spent ten years in Grosse Pointe Park, and Southfield, Michigan where she came to know Gerry LaFemina and his wife, separately, and before they knew each other. She has taught the joys and intricacies of literature and poetry all her life, to people of all ages in universities and schoolrooms, for the Writer's Voice, the New Jersey State Council on the Arts, and a variety of institutions for young adults, including now, to seniors, both privately and in the Evergreen Forum, an organization dedicated to life long learning. She has been known to work in kennels and nurseries when not in classrooms or tending grandchildren.

Elizabeth Socolow's *Between Silence and Praise,* was published by Ragged Sky Press Poetry Series (2006). *Laughing at Gravity: Conversations with Isaac Newton* (Beacon, 1988) won the Barnard Poetry Prize in 1987. She is the mother of grown sons and has lived and taught in New Jersey and Michigan, with and without them and the presence and the ghosts of various wonderful cats and rooms full of plants, ferns, and flowers.

Spirituality Is a Companion

Spirituality is a companion of solitude, an offshoot of being in steady conversation only with oneself in most of one's waking hours. It springs of the time to remember dreams, the silence of days, the return of chance observation. Born of necessity, it becomes practice and habit, enlivens time and space, fills loneliness with warmth, interest, communion, the deep, quiet answer of plants. It is a way of life that was given to me as answer for what I never would have chosen or recommended: living alone. It is what makes the daily occasion of my adulthood bearable. It is the aspect of myself from which I can give something of calm and joy to others.

Thank You Note to the Guests

Thank you for seeing the fountain in the blue fescue,
how long grass imitates water,
as we imitate our mentors and teachers.
Thanks, too, for not minding the overcooked potatoes,
and the absence of washcloths in my domestic storehouse,
for liking the corner cabinet I took from the kitchen long ago
to the bathroom of a house built without closets before the civil war,
slavery band this century of invisible walls you have fought so long in
Detroit.
In 1840, when those pine boards in the back room you loved were
laid down,
Whitman had not yet written about his leaves of grass, none of my cats
had been born or died, this last one, ashes buried under the leopard grass
meaning, at last you could visit. How can I say even your headache
(from the wine, not the cat) and finding you aspirin,
which I have not used in years, brought me gladness?
To give so concrete a comfort to an adult, is like holding fretful
hope or a baby for hours, not once remembering the many chores
unaccomplished. The celery will never look the same
since you thought it an exotic plant under the loosestrife,
bleeding its maroon come-hithers, not yet gone to seed and turned to green;
and the image from your dream—
I, holding my celery-scented hands to the one I imagine pleasing,
he burying his face in the leaves, gave me a premise of hope
I cannot allow myself, unless I falter,
dream being so different from waking.
There is no instruction in our well mannered childhoods
for such notes of gratitude, nor any mention of what a solitude such as mine
might come from. How I long, not tethered enough by work,
to find this floating place of my self an anchor,
all unmoored without you, not family, not lover.

Maintenant, A Present that Inclines Us to One Another's Light

My great friend speaking of flowers, writes:
here's a gift to reclaim the dark solstice,

a present that inclines us
toward one another's light.

And that is the present I want,
so intense only the light of the Other
is known: the walls grow dim, the scent
of paper whites like a memory.
I mean the gift of Now, as I think
my friend may have, at least in some part
of herself, given as a gift to all of us
to rediscover, the present
held in the hand as the French have it,
main tenant, the present held in
the familiar place, hand
not filled with anxiety and regret,

a kind of western Nirvana, not eased into
by meditation and long practiced
alpha rhythms, but come upon for what it is
to look you in the eye, dear ones, each I love,
who insists on being absent. I hold you
in my glance, your light that inclines me
to feel alive in what is, this moment that might
extend, but is relieved of travel,
held in the hand, this present now, this gift,
this glove of life in which we turn, this prayer.

Order, Like the Sequence of the Seasons

Like the sequence of the seasons,
and the perpetual, unseen motion of this globe
our earth, turning in the heavens, shifting its spinning
spine toward the sun and away, so that beyond us,
only guessed at by us, are mysteries we can call God,
we offer imitations of order,
as winter moves to spring, given in thanks
for the counting harmonies around us.

At this, our paschal, season, we see again

the breathing holes in matzo,
the protective shells of things,
the egg, its new life, springing—
the green things, fiddleheads unfurling,
grass spiking toward the sky,
buds bursting on trees, from the seeds
of their breathing spots on branches,
blossoms holding seeds, the little lambs, freed
like us, from long confinement.

Permanent Boarders

Cactus: Sculpted: forms so astonishing in air,
Sonoma desert mesas leaning against the sky and earth—
was I ever a disturbance in space?
agave, prickly pear, how they give food, rope, drink
pressing thorned and buttoned humps
into the parched wilderness of no camels.
The way the fingers of cactus grow,
building as all plants do, on what is already known as form
—mildly comic in this wildly variable climate—
not lush like ferns, with their regular repetitions,
musical as repeated triplets, fugue—
the spines on cactus are dessicated leaves.
I stand here in the supermarket
among tooth-rotting candy and coated nuts
surveying the garden corner
feeling only gratitude for the original created world.
In my selection of this week's prayer-as-plant,
I am witness to candor of the spirit
like a friend who believed that absence
and generosity could be expressed in white walls,
white desk, white table, chairs.
Student of the roots of words she knew *candidus-a-um*,
a clear spreading openness—not a blankness.
Any more than the desert is an emptiness, source
of these small plants I can't resist, bring home
with the juice and bread and eggs, each one so loved

even before acquired, they are like an offering
to hope not of my making.
                                        Which might be enough
were it not that any live thing that enters a home,
fully seen, known, will draw away the breath,
like this latest small wonder, a three stemmed miniature
seguaro, or what could pass for such,
pressing its columns in a kind of praise
of light and life and air.

Letting in the Light

Curators, with their Roman title, care for things,
small scraps of leather on which rent receipts
were written before paper was commonplace.

Call it love that lights up the face of those whose hands
in explanation shape the off-square bits of what once
was cow or sheep or horse, bent at the edges, inscribed
with the accounting. Such numbers in our lives
are as important as idea, haiku, some chance remonstrance
against lost love or rain, brief celebration, after all,
of such a joy as this: an object and a custom carried
here to this bound box across four centuries or more.
And that might be enough, the curiosity, the curator
his white hair, chair on wheels moved toward me,
both of us warming to his knowledge, his apology
for his ankle that did not let him stand.

He wants to let me know the Books of Hours were
sometimes ill-written with inkblots and ungainly shapes
in the illuminations, and they knew the difference.

The beautiful ones preserved the gold-laced
pictures with a kind of vellum, translucent as the appeal

from charities that open up your purse. The light shines
through. The print on that pliant window seems like
writing on still water. The man says the name
was uterine vellum fashioned from the skin of unborn
calves. And I sit hoping accident bred such knowledge,
no cow killed for the soft loveliness of the still
swimming calf's skin, instead each bit
of the slaughtered creature put to use, then,
when, paper was scarce as lasting love
and even peace-time butchers knew

we are curators of all creation,
every kind of holding stuff that comes to hand.

Alone with Roses

At sixty, I planted the first bed, and they tentatively said *yes,*
and then more each year, till prayer augments and I see thorns
and think only of daring to persist and the color of more roses,
of love itself calling to the bees who come.
And had I not been alone with roses, I think I would still have read like this,
and been compelled to write, though my subjects might have been different,
I would still have wanted somehow to tell
the immerson of all being through the eye,
to have known, as I do, the mystery of that seizure—
a book's pages forcing childhood's newness on me, every time,
remembering how to read, remembering how it suddenly made sense,
the moment of seeing the letters become something else,
beyond letters, as I watched so many moments
of my father's diminishing connections, the brain's links uncurling.
How does it know how to wind— the wild clematis
insinuating its pendulous white legato on the white fence?
How does the walnut learn meat from shell,
the fine skin veined with life, adhering like goldleaf to the kernel?
I say, I still would have heard the thrill of that scat soprano voice
meld note to chord and blend itself back on one word,
or the dog joy at the door when I come to use the long leash and trot

beside
in place of my neighbor's currently slowed, gimpy leg.
And had I not been with the roses like this, on my own,
I still would have seen the way there are too many reds
to trust even a baby's quilt will match the rocking chair cushions
with their yolk yellow piping. I would, surely, have still learned:
to discern a good painting from schlock, to know "schlock," "kitch,"
"klezmer,"
the great words imported and alive from my decimated people;
and to go on visiting my mother in the city, in spite of bridges that may,
at any moment, be exploded by others who hate.
And it may be that if there had been someone, and not roses,
on the other side of me, I might not have been so assailed
at the early deaths of those I loved, and those whose books I devoured.
So many dawns of digging, weeding, watering, watching,
I might have lingered in bed, or felt escape's call, rather than
the quiet beckoning of a companion garden. Sometimes, I admit,
I yearn for something more ironic than roses,
kinder than washcloths or luxury soap.
But then I consider that roses have no tongues,
cannot ask cascades of questions, only droop, drop petals,
cannot lecture me on failures and my backward understanding
of digital systems beyond gardener's gloves.
And surely, more comic, at the ballet,
not having been so long alone with roses,
I might have stared with less inquisitive adolescent prying
at the bodies of the male dancers,
so apposite to and opposite of
my own shape.

Cathy Song

Biographical Sketch

Cathy Song of Chinese and Korean descent was born in Honolulu, Hawaii, in 1955,and maintains a permanent home there with her husband and two children. She is the recipient of an NEA Fellowship, the Shelley Memorial Award from the Poetry Society of America, a Hawaii Award for Literature and a Pushcart Prize.

Her first collection, *Picture Bride* (1983), won the 1982 Yale Series of Younger Poets Award and was nominated for a National Book Critics Circle Award. Other collections include *The Land of Bliss* (Pittsburgh, 2001), *School Figures* (Pittsburgh, 1994), and *Frameless Windows*, *Squares of Light* (Norton, 1988).

Statement

As a human being, a Buddhist, and a poet, I am in a usual state of conflict for the very things that arise out of being human are the very things that need to be held, examined and refined in the making of a poem and, at the same time, extinguished or at least minimized to ease suffering. Take, for example, the voice, the speaker, or the maker of the poem, all of which establishes the fiction that the one who asserts the poem into existence is reliable and solid, that the experiences themselves are reliable and solid. Another example is the realm of emotions, which causes us suffering in life. As long as we have emotions we dwell in human form, stuck in birth and death, our own worst enemies, but emotions are cultivated, prized even, as the generating force behind a poem. There is also the use of the sense faculties. The poet opens wide these sense doors, remaining vigilant to what comes burning through the doors. This brings further suffering for what is perceived through the senses—whether it be through the eye, ear, nose, mouth, skin, or mind—brings discrimination, likes and dislikes, pain and pleasure, and attachment, desire for what is perceived as pleasurable, desire to be free from what is perceived as painful. All results of past conditioning we can't seem to resist as human beings and endless material for the poet to mine. The ideal state of equanimity cannot be established. The reality of impermanence is another point of tension. The poet tries to capture the fleeting moment, resurrect the ghost of the past and hold it still, carve it into existence, yet by holding on to it, whether that moment is one of joy or sadness, excessive rumination results in either regret or longing. Rather than being released and seen for what they are—illusory, transitory—these moments are seen as real and solid as they live on in our stores. These stories cause us great suffering. Out of all this conflict, compassion for the foolish, struggling self emerges.

Waiting for Jizo

Like flies to honey, they followed us, the unclaimed,
through the afternoon streets of Pingyao
before the rain came, their presence palpable
as a multitude of hands reaching out from the walls.
The old city seemed forsaken, its inhabitants
retreating from the heat in the amber
recesses of shops selling aged slabs of beef,
handsewn shoes and statuettes of Laughing Buddha,
deformed like melted candles.
The sound of laughter missing from these dwellers,
inert as the ground itself,
centuries of the living packed down hard as stones.
Devoid of tree and flower,
cheap umbrellas supplied the only color
until children spilled forth from school,
licking icy treats, sucking on straws
for the last sweet drop of pop.
fussed about by attending mothers.
Survivors in the land of the single child
policy, we were witnesses to the cherished ones.

Others came here before us, and prayed.
They cleaned what they could,
sweeping with a surge of devotion
the clouds of bondage
a city as old as this one inherits,
compound, an agitation on windless nights.
In a tiny upstairs room at the De Ju Yuan Guesthouse,
careful not to leave anything behind,
we prayed for Jizo to illuminate with his luminous jewel
the way out of the ruins
for those remaining unclaimed, long after
the greedy ones had left on whatever flaming
boat they could cling to.
The little ones, forgotten in the frenzied
exodus, hid between brick and mortar.
suspended in the timelessness of these crevices.
waiting for Jizo to ferry them to the other side

where loneliness doesn't weep through walls,
doesn't trickle out of alleyways
like an overflowing communal latrine.

The Beautiful Beasts Are Returning

Some are already here,
standing in the ruins of forests
quietly as trees.

They cannot be seen directly
with eyes accustomed to fear.
Their presence goes undetected
while the oil fires flare.

Horns extend into branches,
wings lie flat as leaves.
Patience grows like moss
on hooves that root,

drinking rain that fell
when they roamed peacefully,
holding the gift of the world intact.
Wholesomeness left when they did.

Those who come long after
interpreted that world as myth.
They were the ones who saw
markings on stone
as hallucinations by a crude and tribal mind.

The beautiful beasts are returning.
Some are already here
to lead those without fear
back onto the path of unobstructed being.

They wait in shimmering formlessness
the imminent resettlement.
Fern curled nostrils

breathe in, breathe out.

The excitable bird flit enchantedly,
feathering through the green frequency,
sweet as nectar drawn
from strange bejeweled flowers.

The beautiful beasts are returning.
They are moving out of the trees.

The Body Remembers Itself in Wholeness

Old thoughts, scented with the weight of roses,
drag us back into the body,
the one we remember in happiness,
the paradoxical bliss of being
free of itself.

You remember flying on a horse
with a boy named Rinzin.
Racing past lakes of glacial ruins,
bowls of blue elixir on treeless mountains,
the body pulled away from itself,
a blur of hooves and hair,
feet, fur.

Laughter roped you over the pass
where flags, wind-lashed, bound earth and sky,
bound you to him
as if in a pact, that all other moments
would proceed from this one—
a river of prayers streaming
from the top of the world, a wish
for all beings to be well and happy,
which included you
and all the days of that life
returning to the moment when you
and the boy and the horse were one.

And later, the day ended in the midnight bathing
at the lake, to be returned repeatedly
in the body's attempt to reenter
the way the skin tightened, the bones chilled,
gooseflesh erupting by a boy's proximity.
With nothing between them but cold dark air,
the men splashed on one side
while the women, whispering among their kind,
saw versions of themselves in you.

Hair, teeth, skin, bones grasp
through the shadow world of night and day,
tumbling out of the dream
to enter the same sad turning of the wheel.
Each step, each prayer
like nicks a prisoner makes to mark
time in a cell
seems feeble in the orbit around likebodies,
sheepish and fearful,
unable to reconcile lives working at crossed purposes.

You want to return to a time
when the body felt free of itself,
as if in the familiar confinement
the body remembers the full moon, the lake,
the first of many loves to leave you breathless.

Breaking Karma

Beings flame into existence
in and out of the shadow world,
the one we travel through as real.
On streets, where nothing remains hidden,
the six realms collide.
We see only what we are
capable of seeing.
Flying apsaras appear as pretty hostesses
offering a menu of services.
They vie for your attention

alongside the legless stump of a man
who barks after you, propelling
a torso lashed to a wooden scrap with wheels.
The gods glide by in black foreign cars.
They feast on cat and snake and monkey.
Still the desire for wilder meat is strong.
On streets, where nothing is hidden,
the scarred-skinned survivor of some hellish fire,
ropes of flesh twisted into tourniquets of bacon,
rubs against you,
mocking your aversion.
You can't deny you find
the rawness thrilling,
the multitudes streaming past,
each encounter a chance to make amends.
You light incense at every temple.
Innumerable sticks, flaring, then settling,
burn repeatedly
into the urn of human ash.
The earth is the urn of human ash,
a smudge of pigeon-gray talc,
coughing up one more summer of peaches
in the palm of your hand.

Breaking karma is hardest
with those who are hardest
to love, those closest to us
who wait out our endless return.
Upon arrival your mind whirls with prayer wheels and flags
bargained for at roadside carts, incoherent snapshots,
Laughing Buddha on a keychain, bundles of temple
incense broken into pencil bits of lead,
as if all the sentences constructed
in three-star hotel rooms, greasy
dining cars of sleeper trains and other
grog-filled transit points had seeped down
to a handful of regrets.
You chose to exit, traveling
halfway around the shadow world
to crawl into your own bed,
strangely malnourished.

Those closest to you wait
to welcome you back,
you who are so hard to love.

Gerald Stern

Biographical Sketch

Gerald Stern, the first Poet Laureate of New Jersey and newly-elected Chancellor of the Academy of American Poets, was born in Pittsburgh, Pennsylvania in 1925, the son of Polish and Ukrainian immigrant parents. He received degrees from the University of Pittsburgh and Columbia University and spent his twenties living in and traveling between New York City and Europe. He wrote and published poetry in his early twenties but only began to publish extensively in his middle and late forties, and has since published fourteen books of poetry and a book of personal essays. He has two grown children. Stern lives in Lambertville, New Jersey, a small city on the Delaware River. His companion is Anne Marie Macari, herself a poet.

Gerald Stern's most recent book of poems is *Everything is Burning* (Norton, 2004). He is the author of 14 books of poetry, including *American Sonnets* (2002) and *This Time: New and Selected Poems,* which won the 1998 National Book Award. In 2005 he was awarded the Wallace Stevens Award by the Academy of American Poets. He is retired from the University of Iowa Writers' Workshop.

Role of Spirituality Work

It is difficult to extrapolate a statement about spirituality—as such—from my poems. The "spirituality" is contained *in* the poems and has to do not only with the statement, but with the rhythm, the tonality and the music itself. Spirituality resides in the most unexpected places, a flower, a thought, an act of justice, an encounter with another human being. I suppose—if pressed—I would say that there cannot be any light without goodness, nor any goodness without light. And light is love.

The Thought of Heaven

There is one blossom on my redwood table
I smell for hours, even holding it
like a handkerchief in the palm of my hand
and bringing it to my face. I recognize it
as a kind of thought, as in the black locust
the poor of the world for one or two weeks a year
have their paradise, nor is it disgraceful
nor is it weak and seedy even if the leaves
they love to strip are dry; as in the phlox,
the weightless phlox, the bees drag down, the six
colors of lavender, a field of wild ninnies
growing like grass where there is a little room
beside the road; as in the bridal wreath
that smells like honey, that covers a city with cream,
there is one day for pomp, as in the dogwood
there is one day for sadness, four curled petals
with drops of blood, growing white or pink
in the cold dirt, all the more to be
the contrast, under some maple or huge cherry,
for me a blossom of thought supreme, nothing
in the world like it; as in the colored weeds
on my dashboard; as in the flowers in all five pockets;
as in my blue jacket once I found twenty years
of thought—more than that—the election
of Lyndon Johnson, the death of Eleanor Roosevelt—
look how they are political—Americans
in Lebanon, in Hispaniola; I sit there
like a tailor, cleaning out lint, whatever
lint is, holding a stem in the air, rubbing
a golden flower through my fingers, catching
the spots of light. The sun is on my left,
the poppies are in my driveway, a wild exchange
is taking place in my yard, something between
my dwarf apples; yellow dust is falling
into the sweet-smelling glue—this is thought,
even it it's copulation, it is a tried
and true intrigue, and old flirtation; there are
swollen stamens and green lipstick; Plato

would be the first to forgive me, but I don't think
of forgiveness now these last few decades. I
struggle past my willow; someone has cursed me
with a weeping willow, it is Chinese and grows
in swamps best, that I remember, swamps and bogs,
that and the sycamore; if anything,
I'll turn away; if anything I'll sit
among the broken sticks facing the fenced-in
weeds, revenge on groundhogs; I will stare
for a minute or two at a private flower, that is
enough for one day—who is it wants to sit
forever anyhow? There are two months
left—I should say three—the wind and the sun
will help me, so will water, so will bees,
for all I know, and moths, and birds; ah what
dark thought once rested in our coats, all of us,
dogs and cats and humans, not only burrs,
not only prickles; how it scatters first
and then floats back; that is what they called
a germ; it was Hegelian; I have
to find the pre-Socratic, that is for me
what thought should be, I am a sucker still
for all of it to hang together, I want
one bundle still. When the sweet scent comes from the east,
thought I call it a thought, it is, as it should be,
something that precedes thought—that is a way
of putting it—something that accompanies thought,
but it is *thought* as it drifts down over the Chinese
willow, as it floats above the table
and penetrates my doors and windows; I bow
down to it, I let it change me, that
is the purpose of thought—I call it all thought, whatever
changes you. Dear apple, I am ready.
What is it for you, is it dreaming, does that set you
free? I call a bursting "dreaming," I call
a rage and sundering by its sweet-smelling name,
as if I were a child domesticating
everything within a mile for purposes
of my own rage. There is a thought. It is
if not in this blossom then in another,
in the lilies of our highways, in the great

round thistles beside them, in the black-eyed Susan,
the flower I always bend down for, most of all—
for two or tree weeks at least—in the chicory,
blues with the dust of the universe, a blue
more like lavender—I would call is purple
if I were extreme—I would say the edges
are white from gripping the sky, or they are drained
from so much thought. I call it the thought of heaven,
not too disgraceful for the chicory,
solemn and blue as it is, such is my thinking.

First Light

Sooner or later everyone's eyes are opened
though it is the pain of light for the first one out
I have the most pity for, his voice shaking, the
beams mostly in vertical lines, the daylight
above the wooded hills most critical,
seen as it is through two French doors, a clock
of crazy birds to the right, a rufous-sided towhee,
a whooping crane, an eastern bluebird, North
American birds—on the hour—singing and calling,
whatever they do, though I can see me sitting
inside a house, and how the horizon line,
given the window, is higher, and if it turns out
we were in a valley and those were mountains,
how dark it was and how I'd have to stretch
to see what's left of the light, for all of life
is lowered like that, you start with a brutal lamp
and so on and so on—I would have a hard time
explaining what was opened in my life
and what was destroyed, and how the streaks mattered.

Justice

Only, to hear him scream, you had to know
that he was in the body of the worm
and even the robin could hear the scream, so close
she was to the shaking ground, and though the struggle
was over in less than a minute, the sun turned red,
as you could see between the birches, but that
was just a decoration, a brief statement
as on a gravestone, *Here lies such and such,*
and at the bottom, below a lily, *the worm*
will lie down with the robin, or it was
two carved roses intertwined, or maybe
the sun was more pink, more from shame, it only
lasted a few seconds considering the
size of things, and more and more the hopping
and screaming, whatever he was, however he was
dismembered, and as for justice, it was redder
still, you would say carmine, you would say ruby,
my clothes were red, my neck and face were scarlet.

Apocalypse

Of all sixty of us I am the only one who went
to the four corners though I don't say it
out of pride but more like a type of regret,
and I did it because there was no one I truly believed
in though once when I climbed the hill in Skye
and arrived at the rough tables I saw the only other
elder who was a vegetarian—in Scotland—
and visited Orwell and rode a small motorcycle
to get from place to place; and I immediately
stopped eating fish and meat and lived on soups;
and we wrote each other in the middle and late fifties
though one day I got a letter from his daughter
that he had died in an accident; he was
I'm sure of it, an angel who flew in midair
with one eternal gospel to proclaim

to those inhabiting earth and every nation;
and now that I go through my papers every day
I search for his letters but to my shame
I have even forgotten his name, that messenger
who came to me with tablespoons of blue lentils.

Lord, Forgive a Spirit

So what shall we do about this angel,
growing dizzy every time he climbs a ladder,
crying over his old poems.
I walk out into the garden and there he is,
watering the lilies and studying the digitalis.
He is talking to his own invisible heart;
he is leaking blood.
            The sun shines on him all day long
as he wanders from bush to bush.
His eyes flash with fire, his eyelashes blaze and
his skin shines like brass,
but he trips in the dirt just like any gardener, or grieving poet.
            I watch him walk beside the cactus;
I watch him kneel in front of the wet horsetails;
I touch his lips.
I write all day. I sit beside him all
day long and write the garbled words.
I sit in the sun and fill a whole new book
with scrawls and symbols.
I watch the sky as he talks about the gold leaf
and the half-forgotten ruins; I watch the words
drift from his mouth like clouds.
I watch the colors change from orange to red
to pink as he tries to remember his old words—
his old songs, his first human songs—
lost somewhere in the broken glass and the cinders,
a foot below the soft nails and the hinges.

Marc Straus

Biographical Sketch

Marc J. Straus: I grew up in Brooklyn, NY, where I met my future wife, Livia, the first day of nineth grade. We were married the week I began medical school. Then medical training for 12 years, academia, practice and so on and I didn't begin to write poetry seriously until much later. The thirty-two years caring for cancer patients is an anomalous life. Without poetry I would not have a voice for what I've seen and heard. We started collecting contemporary art immediately, buying new artist's work and this has been a large part of our life to the present. I have two kids and three grandchildren.

Not God by Marc J. Straus, (TriQuarterly Books–Northwestern University Press) is a play in verse that dramatizes a journey through illness. Alternating words of a patient and doctor, these harrowing, eloquent poems form a remarkable dialogue about life and death. It has been produced Off Broadway by The York Theatre and MCC Theater and was the basis of a museum exhibit at Lehigh University. Straus' previous collections, *One Word* (1994) and *Symmetry* (2000) were also published by Triquarterly Books–Northwestern University Press. Straus is a distinguished oncologist and researcher, with nearly 100 scientific publications. He is also a renowned art collector and has curated numerous gallery and museum exhibits. His poetry has appeared in many leading journals including *Kenyon Review, Field, Ploughshares* and *Triquarterly*. He is the recipient of several awards for his poetry, including the Robert Penn Warren Award in the Humanities from Yale Medical School.

Statement

Cancer suddenly appears and changes lives in an instant. It is a disease sometimes cured, often delayed and whose treatment is almost always associated with significant difficulty. My poems have been my voice for both patients and myself—the need to speak about personal struggle, hope, dignity, anger, and remorse—the leveling and humbling nature of disease and desire to survive. An oncologist can become crass and detached or allow that each human being is a noble enterprise and the fight against this disease is scientific and spiritual.

The Bridge (2)

PATIENT:

I was never good at volleyball. I can't
sail. I've never been to Bangkok or Peru.
I've published twenty-two papers on early
adolescence. Mostly theoretical. Like measuring
intellect. Like imagining a bridge that can cross
the Atlantic. Like imagining sound
without my children.

My daddy whispers algebraic equations
to me, ancient paradigms, he says,
taught to him in heaven by Copernicus.
What is its purpose? I ask. To understand
monumentality, he responds.
The bridge has seven layers of titanium cable
bound together by intention

and rooted in recitations. Seventeen
wise men safeguard the structure.
God meditates in the middle tower while
the eighteenth sings lullabies.

Not God

DOCTOR:

I thought to delay the answer, camouflage
it, by waiting until he asked another
question. But he prefaced the question with,

I know you're not God. This is commonly said
to me, second in frequency only to, What
would you do if it was your father, or wife,

et cetera?. I accept this statement of my undeity
to be rhetorical, a mechanism to permit me
to be imprecise, to use phrases like *it depends*

upon many factors and *a range of*. But lately
I'm increasingly tempted to say, How do you know
I'm not God? What gives you such certainty?

Do you say this to your lawyer, accountant,
or mother-in-law? And if I'm not God, then why
ask me a question that only God can answer?

Two Weeks

PATIENT:

A man's cough bounces down the hallway
like pick-up sticks. Three rooms away
an IV machine beeps constantly. I know
the distance by now. I know Mrs. Applebaum
was discharged today and Mr. Singer
died. Not just the overhead intercom blaring
Code Blue, or everyone running to his door.
It was the stillness afterward, the leaden walk
of the nurses. They've seen it before, but death fills
their shoes. They pass the pills in silence
and at the station their conversation is muted.
I asked Angela. She said he was old and frail
and his kidneys failed.
It is more than she should say, but she is kind
to differentiate his circumstance from mine.
I am here now two weeks.

Cancer Prayer

DOCTOR:

Tell me please, how to be cavalier
after twenty years of treating patients
with arrogant adjectives, with verbs
too powerful to be comprehensible,
and nouns with such innocent sounds—
lymphoma, melanoma, breast

cancer—that they shatter my ears.

Hope is sometimes a puddle
of stale rainwater for a parched mouth,
though I must continue to pray.

I pray that the power that makes genetic strands
proliferate aberrantly allows us to reverse it,
to discover a gene insertion to correct
each untoward event, and if not, then just today,
I pray that the little boy with Wilm's tumor
will have no side effects from his chemotherapy,
that this one woman with ovary cancer

in room 1122, will have a complete remission.
The word *cure*, dear God, is always
near my lips, though I have been constrained from
saying it aloud. Allow me at least to think it.

Chapel

PATIENT:

There is a chapel downstairs. I passed it twice
on the way to radiology. No one was inside.
There are twelve wooden benches, a large crucifix
and stained glass above the altar. A note in the elevator says,
"religious services for Jews available on request."
Today a priest came in and offered me absolution.
I think you have the wrong room, father,
I said. He checked his notes, laughed courteously, and replied,
now that I'm here… A few minutes later I was sorry.
What harm is there to accept his prayer? I could borrow
his God for a while.

Pine Nuts

DOCTOR:

Just five pine nuts and my nausea
from the Platinol is gone, a thirty-two-
year-old woman in the chemo room told me
today. A man undergoing similar treatment nearby
offered that wrapping one's face in a hot towel

soaked in mentholated oil works much better.
By now I have heard countless anecdotal remedies
that are probably ineffective except for
their placebo effect. Yet each time I think to
dissuade their use, I have to remind myself

of an incident when I was five. I had fractured
my right forearm against our stoop,
having attempted to ride down its six cement steps
on my new twenty-inch Schwinn. Grandma Katy
washed and then wrapped my badly discolored

skin in a cool compress of honey, tree sap
(from a pine, I presume), and another ingredient
that smelled a lot like cesspool sediment. The pain
disappeared completely, and my bones were set
some three hours later without anesthesia.

Luck

PATIENT:

Here's a good one I saw
on an obscure cable station today.

(I think they mostly interview farmers who see aliens
land in their cornfields and housewives

inhabiting someone else's body.) So this middle-aged
man was saying how he gave up smoking last month

and now his surgeon just told him there's a lesion
in his lung and it's lucky because it's curable.

So this man (I think from Pittsburgh), says, just like
it's lucky for those two kids pulled from

a burning building. If it's lucky, how come
they got second degree burns? How come

they were in the building in the first place? Want to hear
about real luck, he says, staring straight at the camera.

I have this itch under my arm. I'll scratch it twice
in slow circles and my cancer is gone.

Michael Waters

Biographical Sketch

Michael Waters remains a Brooklyn boy despite almost thirty years' residence on the Eastern Shore of Maryland and numerous stints abroad. He is married to Mihaela Moscaliuc and will spend Spring '07 as Fulbright Scholar in her native Romania. He has a teenage daughter, and he and his wife are expecting another.

Michael Waters teaches at Salisbury University in Maryland and in the New England College MFA Program. His recent books of poetry include *Darling Vulgarity* (2006) and *Parthenopi: New and Selected Poems* (2001), both from BOA Editions, and he is co-editor of *Contemporary American Poetry* (Houghton Mifflin, 2006). The recipient of an NEA Fellowship, Individual Artist Awards from the Maryland State Arts Council, and three Pushcart Prizes, he has traveled widely, spending time in Iraq, Thailand, Romania, Costa Rica, Malta, and the Dominican Republic, among other countries.

A New Millennium

Each morning, as the news streams in, I recoil from the fanaticism and irrationality and lies on any side, if sides remain possible. Children are dying. Then I recite this lovely and evocative line by John Logan, "The name of God is changing in our time," to prevent myself from going numb, and to keep a spark of faith, no matter how dim, alive in this new millennium.

Driftwood

God's castoff sculpture on the lesser scale:
forget the riven spines of mountain range or
rubble-strewn calderas thrust above sea level.
Been there, done that, He might sigh. And Who
would compete with His own stubborn creation
wasting a century to spire a single cathedral?
So He works quickly, having read trendy
texts on the art of *not-thinking*, those Zen
tea salesmen who honor watchful ancestors
by pouring ceremonial clouds of steeping
leaves into tiny, ceramic cups, never
spilling a drop. One tear brims God's wide eye.
(Severe storm warnings flash along the coast.)
He has no ancestors due homage, none
to offer Him some thorny branch of wisdom.
So He allows His hands to begin their work,
oak after long-standing oak pared to a knobby
stick, teeth-marked pencil, nubbed
splinter, then begin again, till
the coaxed wood issues forth its primeval
soul, the cacophonous score of the creation
captured in grooves and gnarls. This jazzy
combo of wind and rain—God's callused palm,
His blunt right thumb—conjures now a tulle
fog beachcombers must part in order to touch
what's been tossed along the littoral:
these modest abrasions shape-shifting
with sand fleas, this rank curvature,
the swirling grain's giddy abstractions
beckoning the sidewise crabs who vex
from one knotty installation to the next,
stalk-eyed critics ragging this tidal
gallery of slathered grit, frothing *no Louise*
Nevelson while God sips one more scotch.
Philistines, He fumes, *why do I bother?*
but He won't return to marble, won't ever
go back to clay—why repeat Himself?

He knows the artist has no choice
but to bumble forward, abandoning
each failure as He abandoned the grand
gesture, these crumbling continents, God's juvenilia.

The Conversion of Saint Paul

In 1956 I was the shepherd boy
with nothing to offer the infant Jesus.

Kissed goodbye, I left the walk-up
in a white, ankle-length, terrycloth robe,

flailing my grandfather's wooden cane
wrapped from crook to tip in foil.

Secretaries stared from passing buses
at this Biblical apparition

leading his invisible sheep to school,
O little, wild-eyed prophet of Brooklyn!

Older, I portrayed the leper
gifted with half of St. Martin's cloak

and, with paper arrows and red Play-Doh,
evoked the passion of St. Sebastian.

Then I had to fake a terrible fall
to honor the conversion of St. Paul—

when I changed into costume
in the boys' musty coatroom,

Sister Euphrasia knelt to hike
the elastic waistband of my briefs

to better arrange my torn-sheet toga.
In second grade, this ageless ogre

had pasted Easter seals on my skull
and locked me in a cobwebbed cubicle,

pretending to air-mail me to China
where I'd never again see my mother!

Funny enough today, I guess,
but then I pleaded for forgiveness.

Now her sour breath flushed my face
when—classmates clamoring their impatience—

she whispered Jesus
would be judging my performance,

then thrust me from her failing sight
to be apprehended by all that light.

Christ at the Apollo, 1962

"Even in religious fervor there is a touch of animal heat."

-Walt Whitman

Despite the grisly wounds portrayed in prints,
the ropy prongs of blood stapling His eyes
or holes like burnt half-dollars in His feet,
the purple gash a coked teenybopper's
lipsticked mouth in His side, Christ's suffering
seemed less divine than the doubling-over
pain possessing "the hardest working man."
I still don't know whose wounds were worse: Christ's brow
thumbtacked with thorns, humped crowns of feet spike-split—
or James Brown's shattered knees. It's blasphemy
to equate such ravers in their lonesome
afflictions, but when James collapsed on stage
and whispered *please please please*, I rocked with cold,
forsaken Jesus in Gethsemane
and, for the first time, grasped His agony.
Both rose, Christ in His unbleached muslin gown

to assume His rightful, heavenly throne,
James wrapped in his cape, pussy-pink satin,
to ecstatic whoops of fans in Harlem.
When resurrection tugs, I'd rather let
The Famous Flames clasp my hand to guide me
than proud Mary or angelic orders
still befuddled by unbridled passion.
Pale sisters foisted relics upon me,
charred splinter from that chatty thief's cross and
snipped thread from the shroud that xeroxed Christ's corpse,
so I can't help but fashion the future—
soul-struck pilgrims prostrate at the altar
that preserves our Godfather's three-inch heels
or, under glass, like St. Catherine's skull, *please*,
his wicked, marcelled conk, his tortured knees.

God at Forty

I think God must be reading,
or crumpling love letters, or poking His cramped finger
into the ash of the dead
fire to resurrect the flames and warm His mildewed room.
Rain spatters the cabin roof.
One hushed breeze freshens the crab apple blossoms upstate
where God summers. They're pleasant,
these evenings spent in solitude, though God remembers
each of His former lovers
who steamed exotic meals for wary angels, Thai oil
to relieve the strict boredom
of living with a brooding Being whose creative pulse
drove Him inward, whose silence—
that dour guest— too often graced their bountiful table.
Now God keeps His meals simple,
noodle soup simmered on the single coil, peppered brie
slabbed on chunks of broken bread.
Late afternoons neighbors bring baskets of blueberries,
predict dry weather, then leave.

Near dusk God revises His poems, counting syllables—
traditional forms soothe Him
(though He prefers free verse), lend emotional restraint,
keep Him from stepping over
the border of sentimentality where minor
post-modernists stray. Not God.
His eyes water, the owl's clawed feet loose the poplar branch,
the fire wavers, and He sleeps.
Another shitty day in paradise, He might joke
on scrawled postcards never sent.
And dreams: unclasped bra, sunburnt back, freckled skin peeling.
Ants file the smoke-smudged ceiling.
One mouse scurries from its woodpile shelter, zigzags back.
Then God awakens, opens
His black binder to erase some easy metaphor.
He never answers prayers, but
heeds His morning routine: NPR, knee-bends, java,
then work, always the work, lost
for hours in rough drafts, until the broth boils, the cheese-wedge
flicks its furred green tongue of mold,
or the last loaf crumbles, and God's immense loneliness
overwhelms. He scrapes His pocked,
bristly cheek along the splinter-shot table, eyes shut,
allowing His vast yearning
to wash over the planet, cool scouring blankness, that
leaf-lit, resplendent seepage
whose source He sometimes forgets—within Him or without?
Rain quickens the white dwarf pines.
God's manuscript blows open, thumbed leaves riffling, their chirr
the psalm of His rasped breathing.

Claude Wilkinson

Biographical Sketch

Claude Wilkinson was born in Memphis, Tennessee, and grew up on a farm in northwest Mississippi, the youngest of four. He is a graduate of the universities of Mississippi and Memphis respectively. He has taught in the English departments of a number of colleges and universities.

Claude Wilkinson's poems have appeared in numerous publications, and his poetry collections include *Reading the Earth* and *Joy in the Morning*. Also a visual artist, his work has been featured in many exhibitions. He is winner of the 2000 Mrs. Giles Whiting Foundation $35,000 award, given annually to emerging writers of exceptional talent and promise.

Cold Fusion

Usually my poems explore, or attempt to make more obvious, in lyric form, the fusion between a natural and spiritual realm, between loss and memory, between suffering and consequent change. I spent a lot of my childhood in the woods, and nature has always been very attractive to me; however, my poems are more Christian than they are Romantic because my faith governs my work. Thus the poems ultimately point to the inherent rewards of continuation and survival, of having life and having it more abundantly.

Baptism with Water Moccasin

> *And the Lord said to Satan, "From where do you come?" So Satan answered the Lord and said, "from going to and fro on the earth, and from walking back and forth on it."*
>
> -The Book of Job

His bulk amazed us,
the way he'd maneuvered his folds
onto a switch of elm
directly above the baptizing hole.
After all, Cedar Creek offered
numerous spots for a snake
to wile away a Sunday, but only one
fit to baptize in.

Not even the brilliance
of proselytes, a rite of sheets
fluttering about them
in the early morning breeze,
had moved him. Not the most
floral, feathered, tasseled of hats,
nor the highest notes of a Doctor Watt
being held till the last thread
of their power—
nothing made him so much
as shift that bitter lozenge of a head,
shovel through the chilly fork of his tongue
to even feel us out.

It was as if he already knew
what was going on, as if
he'd been returning for ages
to blaspheme the Creek.

While the deacons
crawfished into place,
one could scan the bank of faces
almost hear people calling up Scriptures,
favorite prophets to deliver us.

The sister in the blue crêpe de Chine
sees Joseph released from Potiphar's prison,
and the old man there
with Stetson still on
is remembering Daniel in the lion's den.
Over there Jonah is being spat up…
Shadrach, Meshach and Abednego.
Everywhere shields were rising,
going forth against the tree.

A few boys with the story
of David and Goliath
burning their hearts
gathered stones to make war,
aimed to chuck the devil down
into the cloudy waters below,
but Pastor Gamble, an old hand
at this sort of thing, cautioned,
"Leave him be, chillun.
Long as he up there,
we knows where he at."

Grail

Every Christmas, while webs
of breath shivered from me,
I bore the icy lesson
of faith: that is, to wait
and keep waiting.

Under a temple
of sycamore and locust,
the flurry-glittered cedars,
I hoped for something different
from ordinary broadcast of stars,
for the already dark sky
to pitch completely black,
except for one remarkable fire—
a shepherd's sign

for me to rise and follow.

What I wanted
was to be changed
from child to a giver
of omens and dreams,
to be led along the fence line
beyond our few head of cows
clamped together against harm,
through paths of burdock,
into a cove filled
with as clear a beacon
as those for Saul and Monet,
some place where
I could've listened
to the sound of
a hoot owl's swoop
down from its tower
through ripples of wind,
or for anything else
even slightly like
the shuffling of angels' wings.

Lively Oracles

What is it then if stones speak
in soft code one to another, if
scarlet, gold and cinnamon leaves
scumble God's message on the hearts
of streams, if wellsprings spool

over their kingdoms of mink
and bream revealing His aim?
What is it when a season's touch
pries a first violet from the scheme
of earth, when a certain air

means the last wink of blooms
should hide like drowsy animals

till the next green blaze—
what then when something that's not
the tongues of a thrush

or jack pines rushed with light
can open the body and change
the course of life? If just once,
there's a stirring that moves
on the blood, someplace where

we wonder who couldn't stay forever,
where we're made to think of swans,
to ask for their perfection, especially
their wings to lift ourselves
as white as the bones of a child.

The Grace of Dreams

With all the possibilities to dream of,
why not that picture of Rousseau's where
lions peek like astonished kittens
through passionflower and fern, where trees
festooned with monkeys and fruit
surround two nudes: one, earthier,
almost hidden in the understory,
pipes a horn as if a muse
for the other's desire; and the other,
as fair as sunlight, reclined
on settee, beckoning to come,
if we can, into her perfect peace?

That, or some other green destiny
blooming at the edge
of my mind, and yet one vision
recurs in biblical fashion,
as when something as occult
as seven gaunt cattle
rising from the river to eat

their fat sisters
grazing in a meadow
warned the king of Egypt
that seven bountiful years
would be swallowed by seven lean.

One soldier's dream of a barley loaf
spilling down the mountainside
and leveling a Midianite tent
spelt the force of Gideon's sword—
as usual, the trial
with a grain of promise.
So maybe even in my field
of only tall bleached grass
and its single leafless scrub,
without breeze or sound
and where nothing ever happens,
hides the favor of the Lord.

Sholeh Wolpé

Biographical Sketch

Sholeh Wolpé was born in Iran but spent most of her teen years in the Caribbean and Europe, ending up in the U.S. where she pursued Masters degrees in Radio-TV-Film (Northwestern University) and Public Health (Johns Hopkins University). Sholeh is the recipient of several awards for her poetry and is the director and host of *Poetry at the Loft... and more*, a successful cultural arts venue in Redlands, CA. She divides her time between Redlands and Los Angeles, California.

Sholeh Wolpé is the author of *The Scar Saloon* (Red Hen Press) and has a CD of poems read to modern and ancient Persian music (Refuge Studios). Her poems, translations, essays and reviews have been published in many literary journals and anthologies in the U.S., Canada, Europe, and the Middle East. She was born in Iran.

Spiritual Journey

For a long time I confused spirituality with religious piety. I looked out into the world through a single window tinted by a single color considered to be that of God's. As I entered adulthood I began to realize that God is like a sketched figure in the coloring book of religions. Each religion uses its own crayons to color Him as it sees fit, then rips out the page from the book, frames it in gilded casings and then proceeds to bow before it in adoration and worship.

Breaking away from the religion I had been taught as a child took courage. It was a good religion, an all-encompassing, peace-loving religion—nonetheless a religion. All religions threaten deserters with various images of hell; some with fire, others with unbearable agony and the more enlightened ones with eternal regret. So as I took a deep breath and began a gingerly sidestep away from religion, I feared unbearable, and surely well-deserved, reprisal from God and his cohorts. But to my surprise nothing happened. In fact, things picked up and got better. I found a whole new world outside my home with the tinted window. Even though I began my journey with a terrible anger towards all organized religions, the rage was necessary fuel to propel me out from religions' sphere of influence. Once outside its gravitational force, I was able to release that anger and turn it into wonderment. That marked the true beginning of my spiritual journey—towards an unknowable creator, my inner self, and eventually towards a spectacular spiritually colorful universe.

I Didn't Ask for My Parents

It isn't like you bend
your dainty spirit neck
down from God's baby-soul-land
and point to a copulating couple
who strike your fancy.

Don't think it works that way.

You are blind-folded
and shot down through heaven's tunnel
into life and where you plop
willy-nilly that's your home.

The Jewish couple may be in the act
at the same time as their Muslim neighbor.

Where you end up
even the cherub who pushed you off
the edge can't know.

We grow up forgetting
our incidental placements
become fond of whatever
bread and religion we are fed.

Listen,

Who has salvation
when we all claim it?

I Was Sung into this World

I came into this world on the same bed
I later slept in as a child.
My aunt, a midwife, large brown eyes
a scar the shape of the sun on one cheek,

sat at the gate of my mother's womb
sang me into this world:

Biya koo-choo-loo, Beeya a-zizam
Injah khayli Ghashangeh, Beeya Beeya
Beeya koo-choo-loo, Beeya a-zizam
Noor ast o avaz, eshgh o mah
Beeya Beeya
Ghal-bemoon shokoo-feh kar-deh barayeh tu
Toolesh nadeh
Beeya Beeya Beeya Beeya Beeya Beeya

Come little one, come dear one
It's beautiful here, come come
Come little one, come dear one
We've songs, light, a kind moon and love
come come
Hearts here have blossomed to receive you
Don't tarry
come come come come come come

It was this song I followed into this world.
Today, yellowed by age and cancer my aunt has a foot in her grave.
I sit by her bed, make her promise to come for me when it is my time,
to sing me into the other life with the same song.

Fragments of a Journey

Father feeds the fire.
Flames leap and hypnotize.
Why venture into the snow?

*****

She squirts ink on her mother's god,
Is told: *Darkness has claimed you.*

She points to the glossy light pulsing

Says: *Look, I'm bathed in truth.*

No, child, her mother shakes her head,
That's The Beloved leaving your soul.

*****

The world is not a merry-go-round.
She axes the horses
Steps off the spinning platform.

*****

A mound of question marks
Allows greater room for oxygen
Than periods and exclamation marks.

*****

Breath at what price?
The air is aflame.

Prayer in Sufi Spirit

Why the braids?
Peace and beauty plaited into one,
hunger into another
the drip-drip of blood from a third.

Beloved,
undo your hair—time for a good brushing
Let your hair loose, let the wind lift it,
each strand curled and free: room for light to roam.

Abdul-Baha

White fezz on his head, hair silver and long
a brown *aba* hangs from shoulders bend
from years of damp prisons, he walks
down the church aisle, heavy on him
the eyes of a congregation who do not yet know
this holy man's claim to God
is only that he is His servant.

Awakening

I lost my faith
the day the horizon's line
focused into a cage's bar.

Something sharp
slashed
my forehead and the pain

Throbs from inside
no physical marks
Our Keeper is clever.

Charles Wright

Biographical Sketch

Charles Wright has published two works of criticism, *Halflife* and *Quarter Notes*. His translation of Eugenio Montale's *The Storm and Other Poems* won him the PEN Translation Prize in 1979. He is a Chancellor of The Academy of American Poets. He won the Pulitzer Prize in 1997 for *Black Zodiac*. His most recent book is *Scar Tissue* (Farrar, Straus & Giroux).

The Stuff of Religion

[My poetry] seems suffused with [the stuff of religion]! I guess because *I* was suffused with the stuff, at such a high pitch, at such an impressionable age, and for such a long period of time—without ever believing it, really—it keeps coming back up on me. As though I had overindulged. The taste stays in my mouth, a taste that is not displeasing to me, but it is not exactly something I anticipate with pleasure. I think that I would probably *like* to believe. I believe in belief, for instance. And it *is* the greatest myth going, isn't it? All those fabulous aspirations and assumptions! I mean, if it *were* true, what could be better? Everlasting life! I'll take a hit off that, thank you very much. Just because you don't believe it doesn't mean you don't like to talk about it, or think about it. Besides, I *do* believe in the efficacy of things unseen. It's just that I don't believe in this particular one. And there's no point in just believing in the trappings, in the manifestations. Flannery O'Connor was right about that, I think—if it's just a metaphor, the hell with it. Or words to that effect. I mean, what could be better than being raised incorruptible in the body like St. John?

Even though I don't have anything more to say, I feel as though I *should* say something else. I mean I'm sort of surprised myself it should seem so suffused with this stuff. After all these years of running away from it so hard, it's rather perplexing to find that it's invaded my subconscious like the invisible worm that flies in the night. Well, so be it. I guess if one considers, as I do, the true purpose of poetry to be a contemplation of the divine—however you find it, or don't find it—then it isn't so strange that my work is so suffused with the *stuff* of religion. We take the vocabulary we are given—in my case, Christian—and use it to our own ends. We try to develop and expand what we are given.

La Dolceamara Vita

Autumn is over. The winter rains
Have settled like feathers from wild geese
deep in the trees.

I start my afternoon rote walk, the wet-step and weekend one,
Up Locust Avenue and back down.

The cold-eaten, sap-sunken gold of the maple leaves
Takes in the light and grows big.

The church chimes like empty villages,
ruin-riddled, far away,
Where nobody goes.

The dogwood is redder now than summer's chokecherry,
Sunset sheen like old wax on the steps into the sky,

Rainwater gone, drifting under the streets while nobody notices.
I reach the hospital and turn back.

Behind me, day darkens, in front of me darker still.
If I had it all to do over again, I'd pull the light

Toward me and start to gleam,
and then not gleam, the way the leaves do,
The dying leaves, and the cold flowers.

In Praise of Han Shan

Cold Mountain and Cold Mountain became the same thing in the mind,
The first last seen
slipping into a crevice in the second.

Only the poems remained,
scrawled on the rocks and trees,
Nothing's undoing among the self-stung unfolding of things.

Little Apocalypse

The butterfly's out on noon patrol,
dragooning down to the rapt flower heads.
The ground shudders beneath the ant's hoof.
Under cover of sunlight, the dung beetle bores through his summer dreams.
High up, in another world,
the clouds assemble and mumble their messages.
Sedate, avaricious life,

The earthworm huddled in darkness,
the robin, great warrior, above,
Reworking across the shattered graves of his fathers.
The grass, in its green time, bows to whatever moves it.
Afternoon's ready to shove its spade
deep in the dirt,
Coffins and sugar bones awash in the sudden sun.

Inside the basements of the world,
the clear-out's begun,
Lightning around the thunder-throat of the underneath,
A drop of fire and a drop of fire,
Bright bandages of fog
starting to comfort the aftermath.
Then, from the black horizon, four horses heave up, flash on their faces.

Snake Eyes

The afternoon clouds are like a Xerox of the morning clouds,
An indecipherable transcript,
ill-litanied, ill-limned.

There is no consolation, it seems, there's only light.
Right there, beyond our dark spot.

Imagination is merely the door.
All we can do is knock hard

And hope that something will open it.

Around the corners of the known world,
                                                                      blue stanzas link
The lines of the first great poem, there is no second.

Idleness anchors us.
                                    Nothing accomplished, nothing retrieved,
We're posed like water striders above the secondhand stars.

We have a taste for the untasteable,
                                                            the radiant root of things,
The unimaginary part of what is unimaginable.

We wait between goodbye and hello,
                                                 an ounce of absence, an ounce of regret,
Standing on one foot, whistling a half-remembered tune.

Mystical twos and mojo, God sockets,
                                                                  clouds roll across the sky,
Letting the light come down on some, taking it back from others.

Rosso Venexiano

And here is a photograph of me taking a photograph
Of Holly and me. In 1969, I think,
In Venice,
                    Timothy Hennessey's wretched painting
Behind us, the ornate Venetian mirror throwing us back
Spotted, rejuvenate, shelved in two.

And that's not half-bad, I'd say,
Chihuly downstairs, and Luke Hodgkin, *acqua alta*
Finally out the door,
                                        the schifo from the trattoria
Flushed through the ground floor hallway's side rooms,
The lettuce flats and cardboard wine boxes
                                                          sucked back toward Malamocco.

End of March, thirty-three years ago.
Across the water, in S. Sebastiano, the Veronesi
Are arc-lit and scaffolded,
The Phantom Turk, square-rigged ghost ship,
still moored on the Grand Canal
In from of Palazzo Guggenheim.

Or so we imagined it,
Corvo at large on the damp streets,
Pound on his daily constitutional, as I've said before,
Exhuming the Zattere and Innocenti,
Fluttering candlelike guttering light
At night in the windows high up in Palazzo Barbaro.

Our altered and unreal lives.
How silly it all was, how delicious,
Palazzo this and Palazzo that,
Guardi and Canaletto from every bridge and opening,
The gold-domed Dogana a harsh relief in the winter sun.
Nobody sat on the steps that year,
not I, not anyone.

What else is bereft in the camera's lens, or the mirror's eye?
People, of course, and the future; Campo S. Polo:
sabo, *co fa scuro*, *Gran Balo Macabro*, the poster announced.
Lord, the detritus.
Write, the voice said. *For whom?* came the response.
For the dead whom thou didst love, came the instant reply.

And will they read me?
Aye, for they return as posterity, the voice answered one last time.
Red of Titian's *Assumption*, red of the Doge's fingernail,
Blood red of the *Serenissima*,
Lagoon light, sunset and cloud blaze,
red of the Cardinal entourage.

Words Are the Diminution of All Things

The brief secrets are still here,
                                        and the light has come back.
The word *remember* touches my hand,
But I shake it off and watch the turkey buzzards bank and wheel
Against the occluded sky.
All of the little names sink down,
                                        weighted with what is invisible,
But no one will utter them, no one will smooth their rumpled hair.

There isn't much time, in any case.
There isn't much left to talk about
                                        as the year deflates.

There isn't a lot to add.
Road-worn, December-colored, they cluster like unattractive angels
Wherever a thing appears,
Crisp and unspoken, unspeakable
                                        in their mute and glittering garb.

All afternoon the clouds have been sliding toward us
                                                        out of the Blue Ridge.
All afternoon the leaves have scuttled
Across the sidewalk and driveway, clicking their clattery claws.
And now the evening is over us,
Small slices of silence
                              running under a dark rain,
Wrapped in a larger.

The Gospel According to St. Someone

Reflected radiance, moon envy, we hang outside
Ourselves like bats,
                              clothed in our flash dreams.
Sunset soaks down to the last leaves of the autumn trees.
Under our heads, the world is a long drop and an ache.
Above us, the sky forks,

great road to the left, great road to the right.

Someone will come and walk on his hands
through the dry grass to the altar.
Someone will take the wafer, someone will take the wine
And walk back through gravestones.
Succor us, someone,
Let us drink from your mouth and let us eat from your tongue.

Eternal penny, counterfeit truth, score us and pay us off.
Buried November, read us our rites.
Salvation, worry our sins.
Awake, we all share the same world,
asleep, we're each in our own.
Lay me down, Lord, let me sleep.

Gerry LaFemina teaches at Frostburg State University where he directs the Frostburg Center for Creative Writing. The former lead singer of a New York punk band, LaFemina has worked as a street messenger, bouncer, office manager, and a college instructor at a variety of colleges and universities. His books include *Graffiti Heart* (winner of the Anthony Piccione/ Mammoth Books Prize in Poetry), *The Window Facing Winter*, and *The Parakeets of Brooklyn* (winner of the Bordighera Poetry Prize and published in a bilingual edition of English and Italian).

Chad Prevost was born and raised in San Rafael, CA, and grew up there and in Richmond, VA. He is a writer, teacher and editor who lives in North Chattanooga, Tennessee. A husband to a therapist and father to two young sons, he teaches creative writing and rhetoric at Lee University. He has also taught creative writing, literature and rhetoric at Georgia State University and Georgia Perimeter College. His collection of poems, *Snapshots of the Perishing World*, is available from Word Tech Press' Cherry Grove Imprint (2006). His poetry, non-fiction, interviews and reviews have been published in places such as: *Review Revue, The Journal, Puerto del Sol, The Connecticut Review, The Seattle Review,* and others, and in the forthcoming Abbeywood Press Anthology 2: *Wings and Waking Dreams.* A contributing editor to *Chattahoochee Review*, Chad is co-founding editor of the nationally acclaimed *Terminus Magazine* (www.terminusmagazine.com) based out of Atlanta, Georgia.

Acknowledgments:

*Note: These poems are published here with the permission of the authors and/or publishers who retain all rights.

"The Man and the Wolf" by Francisco Aragon originally appeared in *Maverick.* "Nicaragua in a Voice" by Francisco Aragon originally appeared in *Jacket* and *Tertulia.*

"Yellow Morning," "Pursuit of the Yellow House," "The Name of God," and "Above the Attic of the Yellow House There is Another Set of Stairs" by Robin Behn.

"Keeping My Own Company" and "Star Apocrypha" by Christopher Buckley. Originally appeared in Star Apocrypha © 2001 published by Sheep Meadow Press. All rights reserved. Used with permission of the author. "A Little Poem About God," by Christopher Buckley. Originally appeared in *Sky* © 2004 published by Sheep Meadow Press.

"Prayer" by Christopher Bursk originally appeared in *Places of Comfort, Places of Justice* © 1987, published by Humanities and Arts Press. "De Rerum Natura" by Christopher Bursk originally appeared in *The Improbable Swerving of Atoms* © 2005 published by University of Pittsburg Press.

"Some Heaven" and "Amish Gardens" by Todd Davis originally appeared in *Flyway.* "Prairie Liturgy" and "Prayer Requests at a Mennonite Church" originally appeared in *Image: A Journal of the Arts and Religion.*

"Some say I'm lucky the way I lived through my death" by Travis Denton first appeared in *Slant Review.* "Returning the Indian Pottery" first appeared in *Tulane Review.* "Porter Got Ahead of the Lord" first appeared in *Cimarron Review.*

"Service Station, Tennessee," "My Grandmother Takes the Youth Group to Services," "Ark," and "Sunday Morning" by Camille Dungy originally appeared in *What to Eat, What to Drink, What to Leave for Poison* © 2005 published by Red Hen Press. All rights reserved. "And thou shalt be called a new name which the mouth of the Lord shall name" and "Annunciation" by Camille Dungy.

"Religion" and "Scapegoat" by Stephen Dunn originally appeared in *Riffs and Reciprocities* © 1999 published by W.W. Norton & Company. "Knowledge" and "Here" by Stephen Dunn originally appeared in *Local Visitations* © 2003 published by W.W. Norton & Company. "The Death of God" and "Afterlife" by Stephen Dunn originally appeared in *Different Hours* © 2002 published by W.W. Norton & Company. All rights reserved. "Salvation" by Stephen Dunn.

"Confession" by Stuart Dybek originally appeared in *The Story of the Mist* © 1993 published by State Street Press. "Angelus" and "Benediction" by Stuart Dybek originally appeared in *Streets in Their Own Ink* © 2005 published by Farrar, Straus, Giroux. "Penance" by Stuart Dybek originally appeared in *Brass Knuckles* © 2004 published by Carnegie-Mellon University Press. "Gwiajtska" and "Stain" by Stuart Dybek originally appeared in *The Iowa Review*. "Halo" by Stuart Dybek originally appeared in *Witness*.

"True Confessions," "Proverbs" and "*Rendez-vous*" by Angie Estes originally appeared in *Chez Nous* © 2005 published by Oberlin College Press. All rights reserved. Reprinted by permission of the author and Oberlin College Press. "Chapel" by Angie Estes originally appeared in *Voice-Over* © 2002 published by Oberlin College Press. Reprinted by permission of the author and Oberlin College Press.

"Eve" by Annie Finch originally appeared in *Eve* © published by Story Line Press, 1997. "Watching the Oregon Whale," "Elegy for my Father," "Winter Solstice Chant," "Summer Solstice Chant" and "Earth Goddess and Sky God" by Annie Finch originally appeared in *Calendars* © published by Tupelo Press, 2003.

"And Yet" by Patricia Goedicke originally appeared in *As Earth Begins to End* © 2000 published by Copper Canyon Press. "Unicycles of the Dead" by Patrica Goedicke originally appeared in *Prairie Schooner*. "Aftermath: Pinpoint and Torrent" originally appeared in *Green Mountains Review*.

"Coyote Bliss" by Dennis Hinrichsen originally appeared in *Sou-wester*. All rights reserved. Used with permission of the author. "Viewing the Holy Ghost, Horseshoe Canyon" and "Crazy Horse Mountain" by Dennis Hinrichsen. All rights reserved.

"Thirteenth Apostle" by Mia Leonin originally appeared in *Braid* © 1999 published by Anhinga Press. "Magdalena," "Memory of Fire, and "Mother Tongue" by Mia Leonin.

"And Their Sins Shall Be White As Snow," "And Not For Any Other Name Would I Have Come," "Called to Serve Him," "The Desert Fathers," "Extreme Unction," by Timothy Liu.

"Kansas Grasslands" and "Flint Hills Twilight" by Denise Low originally appeared in *New & Selected Poems 1980-1999* © 1999 published by Penthe Publishing. All rights reserved. Used with permission of the author. "Rough-Legged Hawk: Iowa" and "American Robin" by Denise Low originally appeared in *I-70*. "Kene: Bald Eagle" by Denise Low originally appered in *Connecticut Review*. All rights reserved. Used with permission of the author. "The Bear Emerges" by Denise Low originally appeared in *Grrr: A Collection of Poems about Bears* (Arctos Press, 2000).

"Terese of Avila (1515-82)," "Facing It," "What I'm Telling You," and "My Father's Words" by Shara McCallum originally appeared in *Song of Thieves* © 2003, published by the University of Pittsburgh Press. "The Waves," "The News," and "For Rachel, Just Before Speech" by Shara McCallum.

"Four Psalms" by Allicia Ostiker originally appeared in *The Volcano Sequence* © 2002. Reprinted by permission of the University of Pittsburgh Press. "Approaching Seventy" "In May" and "Dear God" by Alicia Ostriker are used with permission of the author and publisher.

"Palm Sunday" and "In Memory" by Eric Pankey originally appeared in *Apocrypha* © 1991, published by Knopf. All rights reserved. Used with permission of the author. "Homage" and "Homage," "Detail from The Lamentation Over the Dead Christ " by Eric Pankey originally appeared in *The Late Romance* © 1999, published by Knopf. "History" and "My Mother Amid the Shades" by Eric Pankey originally appeared in *Oracle Figures* © 2005, published by AuSable Press. "Let Me Rest upon that Peaceful Mountain" by Eric Pankey originally appeared in *Reliquaries* © 2005, published by AuSable Press.

"In a Glance," "Ambition," "Late Shift," and "Anthem" by Timothy Seibles.

"One Stone to Samadhi," "Peacock," "Clouds," and "Shaking Free of an Epiphany" by Ravi Shankar originally appeared in *Instrumentality* © 2004, WordTech Communications.

"I Have Come to Witness the Sacred" by Vivian Shipley originally appeared in *When There is No Shore* © 2002, published by Word Press. "A Keeper" and "When Your Number's Up" by Vivian Shipley originally appeared in *Gleanings* © 2003, published by The Louisiana Literature Press. "Survivors Have Victims" by Vivian Shipley originally appeared in *Hardboot* © 2005, published by The Louisiana Literature Press.

"Thank You Note to the Guests," "*Maintenant*, A Present that Inclines Us to One Another's Light," "Order, Like the Sequence of the Seasons," "Permanent Boarders," "Letting in the Light," "Alone with Roses" by Elizabeth Socolow.

"Waiting for Jizo," "The Beautiful Beasts Are Returning," "The Body Remembers Itself in Wholeness," and "Breaking Karma" by Cathy Song.

"The Thought of Heaven," by Gerald Stern originally appeared in *Bread without Sugar* © 1993, published by W.W. Norton. "First Light," "Justice," and "Apocalypse" by Gerald Stern originally appeared in *American Sonnets* © 2002, published by W.W. Norton.

"The Bridge (2)," "Not God," "Two Weeks," "Cancer Prayer," "Chapel," "Pine Nuts," and "Luck" by Marc Straus originally appeared in *Not God* © 2006, published by TriQuarterly/Northwestern University Press.

"Driftwood," "The Conversion of Saint Paul," "Christ at the Apollo, 1962," and "God at Forty" by Michael Waters originally appeared in *Parthenopi: New and Selected Poems* © 2001, published by BOA Editions.

"Baptism with Water Moccasin," "Grail," "Lively Oracles," and "The Grace of Dreams" by Claude Wilkinson.

"I Didn't Ask For My Parents," "I Was Sung into This World," "Fragments of a Journey," "Prayer in Sufi Spirit," "Abdul-Baha," and "Awakening" by Sholeh Wolpé originally appeared in *Scar Saloon* © 2004, published by Red Hen Press.

"La Dolceamara Vita," "In Praise of Han Shan," "Little Apocalypse," "Snake Eyes," "Rosso Venexiano," "Words are the Diminution of all Things," and "Gospel According to St. Someone" by Charles Wright originally appeared in *Buffalo Yoga* © 2005, published by Farrar, Straus, Giroux.

Titles in The Harmony Series
Bottom Dog Press

Evensong: Contemporary American Poetry of Spirituality and Religion
eds. Gerry LaFemina and Chad Prevost
1-933964-01-4 240 pgs. $18.00

Family Matters: Poems of Our Families
eds. Ann Smith and Larry Smith
0-933087-95-0 232 pgs. $16.00

America Zen: A Gathering of Poets
eds. Ray McNiece and Larry Smith
0-933087-91-8 224 pgs. $15.00

O Taste and See: Food Poems
edited by David Lee Garrison & Terry Hermsen
0-933087-82-9 198 pgs. $14.00

Hymns and Songs of Purandaradasa
translated by Dinesh Hassan
0-933087-89-6 88 pgs. $12.95

Bowl of Water: Poems by Allen Frost
0-933087-88-8 136 pgs. $12.95

Songs of the Woodcutter: Zen Poems of Wang Wei and Taigu Ryokan
by Larry Smith & Monte Page
0-933087-80-2 (CD & Booklet) $15.00